THE
MEDIEVAL
COOKBOOK

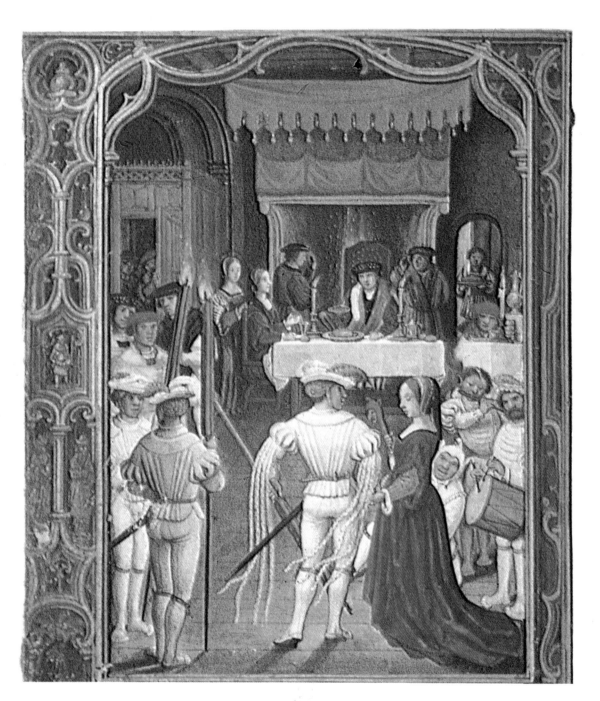

THE
MEDIEVAL
COOKBOOK

Maggie Black

British Museum Press

Published by British Museum Press
a division of British Museum Publications Ltd
46 Bloomsbury Street, London WC1B 3QQ

British Library Cataloguing in Publication Data
Black, Maggie,
    The medieval cookbook.
    I. Title
    641.5
    ISBN 0-7141-0556-2

Designed by Behram Kapadia

Set in 11/13pt Goudy Old Style
by Rowland Phototypesetting Ltd,
Bury St Edmunds, Suffolk
Colour reproduction by Colourscan,
Singapore
Printed in Italy by
New Interlitho SpA, Milan

Frontispiece A torch-lit dance before the
lord at a manorial feast.

CONTENTS

ACKNOWLEDGEMENTS

The scheme for this book came to me through the good offices of Michelle Berriedale-Johnson, and my first debt is to her for thinking of me as a substitute when other commitments prevented her writing it. The confidence she placed in me then has been marvellously stimulating, and I only hope the result does not fall too far short of what she dreamed it would be. The writing has also been a joy, not least because I have been able to work in a museum environment, among people whose way of thinking I value.

Among the contacts I have made, I owe very great thanks to Michelle Brown of the British Library Department of Medieval Manuscripts for the introductory course on medieval manuscripts which she made it possible for me to join last year; and thereafter to Christine Hall who has given me unstinted guidance and help in identifying pictures in the Library collections. My good friend Dr Charles Adams has gallantly helped me to find my needed plant pictures in the Natural History Museum's Botanical Library; I want to thank the staff there too. Similar thanks go to Mr John Goldfinch of the British Library's Department of Printed Books for his help in finding and identifying manuscript negatives. I am grateful, likewise, to Miss Maureen Pemberton of the Bodleian Library, Oxford.

On the cookery writing front, I owe, not for the first time, a very great debt, gladly paid, to the scholar-cook Constance Hieatt, whose transcripts I have used more than most, and who has written so wisely in her books about the problems of medieval recipe interpretation; she has helped her followers avoid many pitfalls. Among my local colleagues, Moira Buxton has inspired me to take a fresh look at several texts I thought I knew well.

One problem almost impossible to avoid is that when several students work from the same few texts, sooner or later they produce near-facsimile results, sometimes relating to a unique and essential recipe. It is chastening to discover that one's own pet 'ingredient mix' or method has been used before, but if it happens, one can only bow and explain to one's forerunner that his or her idea could not be bettered, and beg for its acceptance in one's adaptation. If any recipe of mine is an unwitting copy I ask the original writer's pardon and thank him or her for sharing their work.

I can and do most gladly thank Penelope Ody, BSc, MNIMH, medical herbalist and editor of the magazine *Herbs*, for letting me 'pick her brains' about herbal simples; her knowledge has been generously shared. My long-standing friend Lesley Weissenborn has been more than generous too in letting me use certain recipes which she originally published; and I am also grateful to the author and editor of Mrs Groundes-Peace's *Old Cookery Notebook* and to the International Wine and Food Society for permission to use material in that book which is the Society's copyright. I acknowledge too my debt to Mr Warren Davis, transcriber and editor of *A Leechbook* (MS136), published by Macmillan Press Ltd; and to the Council of the Early English Text Society for permission to use material in *Two Fifteenth-Century Cookery-Books*, *Curye on Inglysch* and *The Babees Book*.

Lastly, I want to thank the kindly people who have made it physically possible to produce the book: my Trojan friend Ewart Wells, who has done much of the recipe testing; Ronald Redfern, who has made my subject index; my ever-patient typist, Judy Stafford, who only once or twice said mildly that she could not read a particular Middle English word (or my handwriting); and above all my editor, Rachel Rogers, who had to cope with a wholly unexpected, unknown author and has done so with grace, wisdom, practical commonsense and charm.

INTRODUCTION

The Middle Ages in Britain are generally said to extend from the fall of the Roman Empire in the West in the fifth century either to 1485 or to Henry VIII's break with Rome in the 1530s; since food habits were closely entwined with religious practices, this book about food takes the later date. The diet of the rich and poor throughout medieval times differed markedly. While magnates and their households had ample fresh and imported foods (except in times of famine) and even in the annual Lenten 'fast' could get fresh substitutes for meat and other forbidden foods, everyone else had to eat mostly salted or pickled flesh foods in winter, and at all the times when meat was forbidden. Moreover, they only had what the local terrain could produce which, at the end of winter or in times of dearth, might be very little indeed.

Although there is no shortage of information on medieval food, the earliest large recipe collections in English date only from the late fourteenth and fifteenth centuries. The adapted recipes in this book are based on ones in those collections; see the Subject Index of Old Recipes on page 141. The material which provides the background to them was written or dictated mainly by literate non-specialists with an experienced and witty eye for human foibles and failings. Three, perhaps four, were senior civil servants or Court officials, and one of these, Geoffrey Chaucer (1340?–1400) had a command of irony and a fluency in literary English unrivalled in his time. One or two had been trained as clerics or in the law. All were fluent in Latin as well as their local English or French. The last section has been compiled from many sources by an unknown hand and recorded by one with little Latin whose prescriptions often either end cheerfully, 'It works; I've proved it' or more darkly, 'Let not the sick know what he is taking'.

As a group, the original authors probably represent a fair cross-section of the intelligentsia in fourteenth- and fifteenth-century Europe. But although their works were chosen more for the objective description of their social scene, the three identifiable single authors, Chaucer, the Goodman of Paris (a rich Parisian writing in about 1393) and John Russell, Marshal to Duke Humphrey of Gloucester up to 1447, also come across as tolerant and kindly individuals.

This cannot be said of most of the characters they portray. There are three types. First, there are the fictional characters who purport to be real folk. Mostly Chaucer's creations, they are distinctly larger than life: the Wife of Bath is larger than most – and her Tale is often accounted the best. Second, there are the flat stereotypes in the fables and folk tales recounted by Chaucer's fictional Companions – tales told by the Goodman too, which every literate adult of their time would know: patient Griselda is typical of the domestic heroines whose mishaps need only be half-listened to as a background to thinking or drinking. Third, there is a group of shadowy but quite possibly real characters, mostly teenagers: the Goodman's child-wife; the boys John Russell was teaching; and in chapter six, the badly schooled, spoiled and vain victim of craftier men, Richard II (1367–99).

The one thing which all these characters, real or fictional, had in common was their unquestioning faith. God was an absolute, beyond doubt – even when they grumbled at, or cursed, the workings of His Church.

The Church's Rules were irksome enough, even in the fifteenth century, although much less so than earlier. Until the early thirteenth century, all healthy adults had been forbidden 'four-footed fleshmeat' on three days a week and in other 'fasting' periods of one or more nights and days. However, the restrictions were respected less and less, and gradually they were relaxed. By the fifteenth century, in

lay society and in many monasteries, only Fridays were obligatory weekly fasting or 'fysshe' days, although Wednesdays and Saturdays might be respected by the pious, and by Church dignitaries in public. Annual fasts such as Rogation Days and Advent were more seriously observed; and Lent, which lasted six weeks then as now, and was the only time when eggs and dairy foods were banned as well as meat, was rigidly kept, at least in name.

Even then, however, the abbot of a rich monastery whose life and business was in most respects like that of any great landowner or courtier, could accept the rich man's standard gift of hunted game for his frequent guests, with whom he ate.

Clerics made up a sizable portion of the population for they included parish priests and wandering friars as well as cloistered monks and nuns. Even after the huge loss of life during the plague of the Black Death in the mid-fourteenth century, a large proportion of the population was still committed officially to celibacy and the dietary rules for clerics. But in the next hundred years, the number of clerics dwindled and their moral force waned considerably. Many monks and even more nuns became frivolous fashion-followers or unashamed gluttons, and the more literate spent hours developing subtle arguments to 'get round' such diet restrictions as remained. The main one that most clerics and laymen alike strove to avoid was the ever-repeated 'fysshe' day diet of salt herring.

Some of the recipes cooks created to titillate the palates of wealthy diners were intriguing and amusing: for instance, the mock hard-boiled eggs made of coloured almond paste dripped into the blown shells and eaten in Lent. But some of the arguments and excuses had cruel conclusions: bustards (large, swift-running birds) and beavers became extinct in early modern England because of men's greed for 'grete fowles' and the specious reasoning that beavers used their tails for swimming so they counted as fish!

There were, of course, plenty of worthy, tolerant and sincere clerics and lay persons. For example, the Goodman of Paris employed Dame Agnes, a woman of the charitable society called the Beguines, to act as chaperone-housekeeper to his young wife. Dame Agnes comes across in his comments as a careful and pleasant guide for an adolescent girl in the new experiences which marriage might

1. Nuns at table, listening to a pious reading. Conversation had to be in dumb show.

entail. It was not uncommon for widows, or other experienced women left alone, to find a useful role in work for the Church such as caring for the young.

The Babees Book, which includes John Russell's *Boke of Nurture*, is not, despite its name, much concerned with very young children. After the editor's forewords, prefaces and notes, it contains nearly fifty short pieces interspersed with five longer instructional poems of various dates, addressed to youths of school-going age upward, including adults who – a modern note – want to live a healthy life. John Russell's is by far the longest of these poems. He himself explains it as the distilled experience of a lifetime 'in service', written down in his 'crooked age' to enable younger men to fill the same role as smoothly as he has learned to do.

So he says in the first verses of the poem where he takes a masterless youth as pupil. But the impression one gains is that the purpose of this teaching material and most of the rest in *The Babees Book* is much wider: how youngsters from affluent homes sent to a great lord's household to be schooled should conduct themselves so that they graduate easily from the status of a page to that of a squire, and then to knighthood.

In Russell's verses we see these lads going through the tasks of every senior domestic officer at a formal dinner, from the cutting of bread for trenchers (slices of coarse bread), table laying and the care of wines to the handling of washing utensils, cleaning and polishing. Some knowledge of nutrition was required, and of the elaborate etiquette of courtly carving, and of handling soups and sauces. Besides this, essential personal hygiene rated high.

Nor was all this merely academic study. Whatever their future role at Court or elsewhere, what the boys learned about running a noble household would be useful. Some lads of lesser degree might well find their metier in such service while others would go home to be carvers and servers to their parents, and would, one day, succeed them as landowners. These lads would have to direct their own staffs and know the etiquette and correct service of food and drink as hosts. One or two might even be called on to act as butler, server or marshal in a formal capacity at a royal or episcopal feast, and gain its magnificent 'perks'.

2. A young squire brings in three piled dishes – to music.

Knights, squires and pages who ranked as henchmen at the Court (whether the king's or a senior nobleman's) were usually fed by the Court commissariat. A young man, on awakening, would wash and dress, and go to the chapel to hear at least part of a mass. Once blessed, he would drink a mug of ale, eat a couple of bread or toast fingers, and go about his planned tasks for the day.

If his lord were going hunting, carts loaded with tables, cushions and baskets and bags of food would already be on their way to some pre-arranged forest dining place. If he were to dine at home, trestle tables would be set up, tablecloths laid and the dresser set with wine cups and jugs, bread board and serving tools. The cup board (a formal dresser with shelves) would be furnished with plate too, especially if there were to be guests. The type and quantity of food served, however, would depend mostly on whether it was an ordinary 'flesshe' day or 'fysshe' day, or some kind of feast day.

Everyone washed their hands before dinner, then trooped to their places to hear grace said. The youngsters at the lower tables cut a stale bread trencher for each person as a plate, and the servers brought round bowls (one between two or four people) for sloppy foods and platters of roast meat or slices of pie. At the top table the lord's carefully cut pile of trenchers was placed before him, and when he took a pinch of salt from his big ceremonial salt cellar, the meal could begin.

The menu was not very grand as a rule on an ordinary day, even in a large household. The lord might have a choice of six dishes in the first course to his senior staff's four, but middle-ranking officers got only three and the juniors two. Everyone could have ale or watered wine although grandees alone were given the wine jar and water pitcher so that they could make their 'mix' as strong as they liked. Only the top-ranking tables got the second course, too, after the tablecloths had been changed; the boys at the bottom end might get a hunk of cheese and an apple to chew while they waited for their superiors, in their fine hats, to enjoy the lighter dishes and pastries, with sweet wine and sugared aniseeds to follow.

Strictly speaking, just an informal snack meal was supposed to be served in the evening at supper. It was certainly more relaxed. The lord and his family or friends usually retired soon afterwards to the private parlour with perhaps a minstrel or story teller to entertain them; and the staff might have one too, say an amusing conjuror or card trickster, before they turned in for the night. Occasionally, though, if the stories were good, they managed to prolong the evening with a late-night snack or *reresoper*, disapproved of by authority but soothing to wine-filled young stomachs.

The preparations for a special feast started early. By noon the display shelves of the cup board winked and glittered with gold and pewter, the best damask cloths lay smoothly over the high table with the sanap (overlay protecting the tablecloth) on top and the match-

3. A picnic by a woodland stream. Everything has been brought including the
table equipment and linen. The wine is cooling in the stream.

ing towels for the servers ready folded. Ewers, bowls and assay tools were burnished brilliantly and so was the best ceremonial salt cellar. Behind and above the lord's chair, his Cloth of Estate glowed with embroidery. Minstrels announced the meal, and the usual preliminaries were followed by the ceremonies of the assay: with ritual etiquette, every dish or drink the lord consumed was touched or tasted first by a servant in case it was poisoned. The proceeding was of ceremonial rather than real value, but it gave the servers time to sort out the seating plan to fit in both visitors and members of the household.

When the whole royal Court assembled for a major feast, every possible dining space had to be used, even barns and dairies, and the complications of precedence were almost insuperable despite there being several sittings. But even a modest feast for a provincial magnate or abbot might mean feeding more than a hundred people of various different grades; and even on a 'flesshe' day, parallel fish dishes had to be supplied for any particularly pious cleric or penitent layman. It was perhaps just as well that only the lord's service consisted of a dozen or more dishes, probably served one by one; the clutter would have been appalling if those lower in the social scale had been given so much choice.

Some clutter was saved by alms baskets on the tables into which left-overs and the helpings of fasting diners were put. After the meal the almoner's staff took them to the waiting out-workers and beggars at the gate. The steward was not allowed to economise by cutting down supplies which would probably not be eaten because some diner was fasting.

The food, although more colourful and varied than usual, was not the outstanding feature of a feast. A celebratory show-piece, called a subtlety, perhaps a sculptured sugar or pastry model, was paraded and presented to the top table at the end of each course; and sometimes there were favours or mementoes for the lower tables too. The main subtlety might be very grand indeed, made in several tiers, each with wax or plaster models in a topical or other setting easily identified by the diners.

The crucial, distinctive aspect of any feast, however, was entertainment, a show. It was not unknown at a royal feast for a noble peer

4. Dancing a
'Carole'.

to present royal gifts in public between courses on his master's behalf. A more common display was a playlet like a revue sketch called (rightly) an interlude, which was fitted in while the cloths were changed for the next course. Alternatively, after dinner, a portable stage or scenery might be wheeled into the main hall, and a play or silent mumming show would then be performed, either by the lord's own troupe or by travelling players. Most great men kept a band of musicians and another of tumblers and mummers to entertain guests, and swapped them temporarily for those of other magnates when bored.

At a small feast, audience participation might be used to prevent boredom, by making guests themselves sing or play the lute for the company: or everyone might dance (a favourite pastime of Richard II which let him show off his fine embroidered clothes). Even clerics in monasteries were said to follow supper with singing, lute playing and dancing with visiting nuns!

A favourite ploy when even dancing and singing 'caroles' (round dance and song routines) palled was to introduce disguisers to add a surprise to the entertainment. Suddenly, without warning, strangers entered the room in fantastical costumes and headgear complete with masks. They joined the dancing, or performed some act or dance of their own in total silence, and then withdrew, leaving the company to guess what they represented, and who they might be. This was, as a rule, not very difficult since they were usually members of the host's household; but the types of disguise and the masks were probably quite a well-kept secret until 'the night'.

'Disguising' was the entertainment in action which corresponded most closely to the visual spectacle and surprise offered by the subtlety in the making of a really first-class feast. These feasts, which like the main and 'mini' fasts punctuated the medieval year, gave the limited diet and usually rather drab labour of medieval men and women variety and highlights, memories to hold and visions of splendour.

To lift their spirits, most medieval people drank well. Ale was the common drink at every meal, cloudy or bright, depending on how long it had stood, and on one's purse; the older and clearer it was, the more it cost. It might be compounded with herbs as the Germans made it (which is how hops came to Britain) or it might be honeyed and spiced and called bragot – which again cost more. Wine was imported too, the newer the better; usually it was drunk watered, and a mark of honour at a feast was to be given the wine and water bottles, to mix one's own.

At feasts, it was commonplace to drink too much; whether at a humble parish affair, or on a grand state occasion when most of the company would have little else to do while those at the 'top table' nibbled last-course sweetmeats. From Christmas until Twelfth Night was always a time of roistering drunkenness; that was understandable. Yet Lent was a bibulous time too, and that could only be explained perhaps by the rigour of the six-week, salt-fish diet.

However, the results were the same and so were the cures. The doctor or apothecary, or the local Wise Woman would be at hand next morning with a remedy for the headache (migraine), the sore stomach and colic, and the flatulence. He or she might then offer a recipe for tooth powder to clean the teeth, or a salve of Rose Oil to calm the nerves; and after that, when the hangover had worn off, the carer might offer the recipe for general good health on page 138 which is as good a way as any to treat the food and drink at a feast.

DAMASK ROSE

I

AFTER DOMESDAY

Even before Duke William invaded England in 1066, there were a good many Normans with power and influence in the land. The last long-lived Saxon king, Edward the Confessor (1042–66), had been brought up at the Norman Court, and when he returned to rule England brought with him Norman friends, counsellors and clerics. Norman barons gained estates in Britain, merchants had moorings on 'London river', and the King's Norman chaplains strongly influenced his way of life. The Saxon nobility deeply resented it.

After Edward died, this led to a power struggle between the Saxon lord Harold who took the throne and Duke William who alleged that it had been promised to himself. William brought over an invasion force and, after his first meal on English soil (graphically presented in the famous Bayeux Tapestry), joined battle with Harold near Hastings. Harold was killed, and William took the throne.

The new king replaced the top aristocracy with Norman nobles, but otherwise left the social structure much as it was, only more firmly controlled by its new masters. These Normans found English households, whether of earls or peasants, monks or merchants, eating similar dishes but plainer and coarser than their own. They at once began importing spices, foreign herbs and other food plants, and even animals (for instance, rabbits); and they introduced upper-class Saxons to their own food tastes, along with elements of their own language. It took a long time – almost three hundred years from

IC:COQVI
TVR:CARO
ET·HIC: MINISTRAVERVN
MINISTRI

5. Making a stew,
and grilling steaks.

the making of King William's grand land survey, the Domesday
Book, which began in 1086 – but by the 1370s a fluent English, part-
derived from French, was being used as a literary written language
and as a medium for recording business and technical material such
as inventories and recipes.

In this first section some recipes from our earliest English-language
cookbooks describe dishes which had not, so we believe, changed
much since the Conquest and the writing of the Domesday records.
We can get some idea of them from the Bayeux Tapestry meal.

Even if this tapestry is a much later work than we have been led to
believe, the sequence showing William dining on arrival is a plaus-
ible early medieval scene. It seems to show quite clearly a hastily

erected camp kitchen with an impromptu hanger for the pottage pot over the fire; and, above it, what looks like a low bed of charcoal in which are embedded larkspits holding cubed and flat meats and small birds. More gobbets are shown on a heater not unlike a Roman sacrificial altar. The chief cook leans over it, holding a flat steak on his flesh hook. Other servitors transfer the spitted meats to bowls, seemingly using their shields as a table. The last scene shows the 'top brass' at table, tucking in to what appears to be steaks (entrecotes?), round flatbreads and perhaps chicken pasties. A servitor kneels before William with what may be a dish piled with frumenty. The spatchcocked small birds (page 33) have not yet arrived; they may be for the second course.

6. Presenting William with a remarkable culinary array.

Frumenty

SERVES SIX

To make frumente. Tak clene whete & braye yt wel in a morter tyl the holes gon of; sethe it til it breste in water. Nym it vp & lat it cole. Tak good broth & swete mylk of kyn or of almand & tempere it therwith. Nym yelkys of eyren rawe & saffroun & cast therto; salt it; lat it naught boyle after the eyren ben cast therinne. Messe it forth with venesoun or with fat motoun fresch. (CI. IV. 1.)

275 g/10 oz kibbled wheat or bulgur (cracked wheat)

1.1 litres/2 pints/5 cups water

150 ml/5 fl oz/⅔ cup meat or chicken stock
or milk (see method)

Salt to taste

OPTIONAL

2 egg yolks, beaten

Pinch of dried saffron strands

Rather than trying to hull and pound whole wheat grain, use pre-prepared kibbled or cracked wheat. Kibbled wheat is coarser, rather like coarse oatmeal in appearance, and it makes a tastier, more nutty basic dish. When buying saffron, try to obtain strands (stamens) rather than powder – you can then be sure that you are getting the real thing. Before pounding or soaking saffron strands for use in a recipe, dry them for a few minutes in a low oven (or for a few seconds in a microwave oven): they will then give out their gorgeous regal colour more readily.

Boil the wheat in the water for 15 minutes or until it softens. Remove from the heat and leave to stand for another 15 minutes or until almost all the water is absorbed. Add the stock or milk (depending on whether you will use the frumenty alone as a basic porridge or whether it will be a side dish or standard accompaniment to venison, porpoise or beef). Bring the liquid to the boil, add salt if you wish and stir over low heat for a few minutes longer. This plain frumenty (often made with barley instead of wheat) was what the Saxons usually ate.

For a richer dish, suited to the tastes of their Norman masters, stir into the prepared frumenty 2 beaten egg yolks and a pinch of dried saffron. Stir over low heat without boiling until the egg thickens slightly. It will thicken more if allowed to stand, off the heat, for 5 minutes before serving.

This was the standard dish eaten with venison by great lords and senior clerics. It was also a symbolic dish in winter, a sign that spring would return.

It still makes a good side dish to eat with strongly flavoured meat and game dishes. But plain frumenty is best today as a breakfast porridge.

Girdle 'Breads'

MAKES SIX

Cruste Rolle. Take fayre smal Flowre of whete; nym Eyroun & breke ther-to, & coloure the past with Safroun; rolle it on a borde also thinne as parchement, rounde a-bowte as an oblye; frye hem and serue forth; and thus may do in lente but do away the eyroun, & nym mylke of Almaundys, and frye hem in Oyle, & then serue forth.
(Harl. 279. p.46.)

¼ teaspoon dried saffron strands

2 tablespoons boiling water

225 g/8 oz plain white flour

Pinch of salt

Knob of lard or butter

2 eggs

Lard for frying

Steep the saffron in the boiling water until the water is deep gold in colour and has cooled. Sift the flour and salt and rub in the fat until the mixture is like fine crumbs. Beat the eggs with the saffron water and use to bind the flour, making a firm but not dry dough. Add extra cold water if needed. Roll out the dough thinly and cut it into 12–15-cm/5–6-inch rounds, using a small plate as a guide. Thinly grease a girdle or large heavy frying-pan with lard. Add the dough rounds, one at a time, and fry on a moderately hot surface, turning once, until browned on both sides.

7. Frumenty and bread for supper.

Spit-roasted or Grilled Steaks

SERVES SIX

To make Stekys of venson or bef. Take Venyson or Bef, & leche &
gredyl it vp broun; then take Vynegre & a litel verious, & a lytil Wyne,
and putte pouder perpir ther-on y-now, and pouder Gyngere; and atte
the dressoure straw on pouder Canelle y-now, that the stekys be al
y-helid ther-wyth, and but a litel Sawce; & then serue it forth.
(Harl. 279. p. 40.)

6 fairly thin beef steaks

Oil or fat for grilling

BASTING SAUCE

2 teaspoons red wine vinegar

1–2 tablespoons Seville orange juice

4 tablespoons red wine

Pinch each of ground black pepper and ginger

GARNISH

Sprinkling of ground cinnamon

8. Here, fat birds are being basted as they roast, in much the same way as on the grill.

Nick the edges of the steaks, and grease them. Mix the sauce ingredients in a jug, adjusting the proportions if you wish. Then grill the steaks as you prefer; warm the sauce, and sprinkle a few drops over the meat while grilling it. Serve the steaks lightly sprinkled with cinnamon and any remaining sauce.

The original recipe calls for verjuice, a popular medieval condiment made from specially grown or (in England) unripe grapes. But another recipe – that of the Goodman of Paris (page 68 ff.) – suggests using the juice of Seville oranges. If you can get these in season and freeze them, use their juice as a substitute for verjuice: it makes a delicious sauce.

Variation: Lamb Kebabs

700–900 g/1 ½–2 lb lean lamb,
cut into 2.5-cm/1-inch cubes

1 quantity of Basting Sauce (see page 26)

There is no original recipe for kebabs as such, but you can follow the
first instruction for Mounchelet (see page 31) and then divide the
cubes of meat equally between six skewers. Grill and sauce the meat
as in the recipe on page 26, using a little more sauce if necessary.

Sweet-sour Spiced Rabbit

SERVES SIX

Egurdouce. Take connynges or kydde and smite hem on peecys rawe, and fry hem in white grece. Take raysouns of coraunce and fry hem. Take oynouns, perboile hem and hewe hem small and fry hem. Take rede wine and a lytel vynegur, sugar, with powdour of peper, of gynger, of canel, salt; and cast therto, and lat it seeth with a gode quantite of white grece; & serue it forth. (CI. IV. 23.)

6 wild rabbit joints (hind legs or saddle)

3 medium onions

75 g/3 oz pork dripping or lard

50 g/2 oz currants

275 ml/10 fl oz/1¼ cups red wine

25 ml/1 fl oz/⅓ cup red wine vinegar

15 g/½ oz granulated sugar

¼ teaspoon ground black pepper

⅓ teaspoon ground cinnamon

⅓ teaspoon ground ginger

Salt to taste

1½ tablespoons soft white breadcrumbs
for thickening (optional)

Although the old recipe starts with a fry-up in plenty of fat, oven browning (a less fatty method than frying) suits our taste better today. Other recipes for this dish add a breadcrumb thickening, so I have provided that choice too.

Pre-heat the oven to 230°C/450°F/Gas Mark 8. Meanwhile trim the rabbit joints neatly. Peel the onions and put them in a pan of cold water. Bring to the boil on top of the stove, cook for 3–4 minutes, then drain. Chop and set aside.

9. Rabbits imported by the Normans soon made themselves at home.

Arrange the joints in one layer in a pot-roasting pan, and smear with the fat. Place the pan in the oven and sear the meat for 15 minutes or until well browned, turning once. Add the chopped onions and the currants for the last few minutes and turn them in the fat.

While browning the meat, mix together the wine and vinegar and stir in the salt, sugar and spices.

Pour off any excess fat in the pan, then pour the wine mixture over the meat and onions. Reduce the oven temperature to 180°C/350°F/ Gas Mark 4. Cover the pan and cook for 30–45 minutes or until the rabbit is tender; uncover and baste occasionally with the wine mixture. Shortly before serving, stir in the breadcrumbs, if you are using them.

If you prefer, you can transfer the contents of the pan to a flameproof casserole before adding the wine, and do the low-temperature cooking on top of the stove.

Lamb or Mutton Stew

SERVES SIX

Mounchelet. Take veel other[wise] motoun and smyte it to gobettes.
Seeth it in gode broth; cast therto erbes yhewe gode won, and a quantite
of oynouns mynced, powdour fort and safroun, and alye it with ayren
and verious: but let it not seeth after. (CI. IV. 18.)

900 g/2 lb boneless stewing lamb or mutton

425 ml/15 fl oz/2 cups chicken stock

2 medium onions, peeled and finely chopped

1 tablespoon chopped parsley

½–1 teaspoon each fresh rosemary leaves, thyme leaves, and savory or
marjoram leaves, bruised in a mill (use fewer dried herbs)

¼ teaspoon each ground ginger, cumin and coriander

Salt to taste

225 ml/8 fl oz/1 cup white wine

2 eggs

2 tablespoons lemon juice

PARSNIP

NTVR :   HIC : EST : VVAD AR

10. The requisitioned sheep held by the Norman soldier is destined for the pot.

Veal can be used in this recipe, but the animals shown in the Bayeux Tapestry appear to be a sheep, a pig and a scrawny old ox.

Cut the meat into 5-cm/2-inch cubes. Put the stock into a stewpan and bring to the boil. Add the meat and bring back to the boil. Skim if needed, then add the prepared onions, herbs, spices, salt and wine. Reduce the heat, cover the pan and cook gently until the meat cubes are cooked through and tender (1–1½ hours). Beat the eggs with the lemon juice until blended, then take the pan off the heat and stir the egg mixture gradually into the stew to thicken it slightly. Do not reboil.

Grilled Quail

SERVES SIX

Quayle rosted. Take a Quayle, and sle him, And serue him as thou doest a partrich in all Degre . . . .
(As for partrich) roste him as thou doest a ffesaunte in the same wise . . .
(As for ffesaunte rosted) . . . pull him dry, kutte away his hede and the necke by the body, and the legges by the kne, and putte the kneys in at the vente, and roste him: his sauce is Sugur and mustard.
(Harl. 4016. p. 79.)

6 prepared quail

Salt and pepper

Melted butter or other fat

Split the birds along the back and beat them to flatten them as depicted in the Bayeux Tapestry. Thread a wooden kebab skewer through each bird lengthways, then secure the quail in shape by pushing another wooden skewer at right angles to the first one, through the wings and also through the legs. Season the birds well, brush them with melted butter or other fat and grill for 16–20 minutes, turning once or twice.

11. Spatchcocked small birds straight from the grill.

2

CHAUCER'S COMPANY

When that shrewd cosmopolitan civil servant and author Geoffrey Chaucer was planning his greatest book, *The Canterbury Tales*, he decided to make it a travelogue 'with a difference'. He would begin with satirical sketches of a varied group of English folk, bound to stay together on a journey, who would each then tell one or two tales in his or her own vein on the way. The result is a brilliant gallery of portraits, of about thirty assorted people.

Since it was a pilgrimage on which they were bound, although a short easy one, a good many were clerics. Among the ones we know best are the worldly, genteel prioress with her entourage, a stout monk given to hunting and 'modern' good living, and a friar who backed his begging with trifles and songs for girls, and with pardons for merchants' wives if they paid for their sins in silver. A pardoner and a church-court summoner were equally mercenary, in contrast to the poor parson who stayed with and sustained his rural flock.

The laity were just as diverse. The most notable was a knight newly back from war, accompanied by his amorous, coxcomb son. After him came an elderly member of the landed gentry who kept open house, being a great and greedy gourmet; his entertaining supported his roles as JP and sheriff. Less well placed were a merchant whose fine talk never gave away that he was 'in the red', an unemployed conveyancer who talked likewise, and a perennial student who spent anything he got on books.

Some of the craftsmen in the party were tough characters: the

12. Canterbury pilgrims on the road.

34

coarse but skilled cook whose dishes we shall try; the 16-stone miller, wrestler and teller of coarse tales, but subtle at fingering and thieving grain; and the illiterate yet wealthy manciple and reeve who knew where to find a bargain, whether buying now or dealing in futures. There is a dishonest doctor who will appear again in chapter eight. Best known of all is the much-married weaver-woman of Bath, with her ribald stories of how to handle husbands.

The stories these characters told were mostly well-tried favourites, each new teller putting his or her own gloss on its events. Some, however, were new; Chaucer himself may have contributed *The Canon's Yeoman's Tale*. Others (the less seemly ones) were tavern talk. Yet others were of classical origin, or from the lives of saints. But all were rooted in real life by the touches Chaucer's own genius gave them – his comments on, for instance, their preferences in women, in dress and in food. The franklin's breakfast of bread and wine, the monk's hunted hare for dinner, and the rich prioress's dainty treats of white bread for her little dogs! The cook's specialities are there too – 'standing' pottages such as 'blancmange' and tasty pies. You will find all these dishes among the recipes in this book as well as others which the pilgrims would have tasted on their way to Canterbury.

BORAGE

White Bread and Rolls
MAKES 2 ROUND LOAVES AND 8–10 ROLLS

We have no recipes for medieval breads, but we know their names and uses as well as Chaucer's miller did. The finest, whitest wheat flour, boulted several times, made bread called wastel or paynedemain (demesne bread). This is what the prioress fed to her dogs. The only finer flour was the wheaten type used for the light pastries called simnels and cracknels, or wafers (the sacramental Host consisted of these delicate white wafers.) The yeast and ale in the recipe below replace the medieval ale-barm used for raising dough in the old days.

1.3 kg/2 lb 14 oz unbleached strong white flour

50 g/2 oz rice flour or cornflour

1 tablespoon salt

25 g/1 oz fresh yeast

575–850 ml/1–1½ pints/2½–3¾ cups warm water

175 ml/6 fl oz/¾ cup brown ale

4 teaspoons warmed clear honey

A little oil for greasing

Mix the flours and salt in a warmed bowl. Blend the yeast to a cream with a little of the water, then mix in the ale, honey and a scant 575 ml/1 pint/2½ cups of the remaining water. Stir the liquids into the flour mixture and mix to a firm dough, adding more water if it does not cohere. On a board or work-top, knead the dough for about 8 minutes or until it feels elastic. Shape it into a ball. Oil the inside of the bowl, return the dough and cover it loosely with oiled grease-proof paper. Leave in a warm place to double in bulk.

Punch down the dough and cut it in half. Shape one half into two equal-sized round loaves and the other half into rolls. Make a cross-cut in the top of each loaf. Place on oiled baking sheets, well apart, cover loosely with oiled greaseproof paper and leave to 'prove' in a

13. Fine white bread rolls or 'manchets' (small loaves) being baked in quantity.

warm place. Meanwhile, pre-heat the oven to 230°C/450°F/Gas Mark 8.

The rolls will be ready first. When swollen and puffy, bake them for 15–17 minutes. Tap one on the bottom; it should sound hollow if cooked. Bake the loaves when ready for about 25 minutes; test by tapping. If not yet done, bake for a little longer at 150°C/300°F/Gas Mark 2. When cooked, leave to cool, covered with a cloth, on a wire rack.

Bread baked on metal sheets tends to have a hard crust. If you cool it covered, you prevent steam escaping so the bread stays softer. You can, if you prefer, bake the loaves in two oiled deep cake tins with removable bottoms, to get a softer crust.

Braised Spring Greens
SERVES SIX

Spynoches yfryed. Take spynoches; perboile hem in sethyng water. Take hem up and presse out the water and hew hem in two. Frye hem in oile & do therto powdour douce, & serue forth. (CI. IV. 188.)

700 g/1½ lb small whole heads of
spring greens or spinach

3–4 tablespoons frying oil

¼ teaspoon each sea salt, freshly ground black pepper,
grated nutmeg and ground cinnamon

Small sprinkling of soft light brown sugar

Spring greens are probably closer to medieval spinach than our modern spinach, but the recipe is good made with either. Our forebears would probably have used rape oil for this dish, most likely imported from Flanders, but King Richard's cooks could certainly get hold of costly nut or olive oil with its finer flavour. I have added a little stock or water to the frying oil because the first tests gave very greasy results.

SPINACH

14. Nutmeg was valued as a spice in vegetable dishes, sweet dishes and mulled drinks alike.

Wash the heads of greens or spinach and trim off any stems. Bring about 5 cm/2 inches water to the boil in a large pan and put in the heads side by side; if they do not all fit in, blanch them in two batches. Turn them over with two wooden spoons for 2–3 minutes until softened. Cover the pan, lower the heat and simmer for 5 minutes.

When all the greens are blanched, drain them, reserving any liquid left. Squeeze the heads dry in a cloth and split them in half lengthways. Heat the oil in a deep heavy frying-pan, then add the wilted greens and about 5 mm/¼ inch of the reserved cooking liquid or water. Add the spices and sugar. Turn the heads over to coat them with oil, cover the pan and simmer the contents until the ribs and stem ends are tender. Serve in a warmed dish with the cooking liquid or not, as you please.

Golden Leeks and Onions
SERVES SIX

To make blaunche porre. Tak whyte lekys & perboyle hem & hewe hem smale with oynouns. Cast it in good broth & sethe it vp with smale bryddys. Coloure it with safferoun; powdur yt with pouder douce.
(CI. IV. 2.)

1 teaspoon dried saffron strands

2 tablespoons boiling water

6 medium leeks (white part only)

3 medium onions

575 ml/1 pint/2½ cups chicken stock

⅓ teaspoon soft light brown sugar

Good pinch each of ground white pepper, cinnamon and cloves

Yellow food colouring (optional)

The summoner in Chaucer's company loved onions and leeks, so he would have enjoyed this dish, even without 'smale bryddes' (black-birds or finches) in the pot.

First, soak the saffron strands in the boiling water until the water is deep gold. Prepare the leeks by trimming the root ends and slicing the white stems into thin rings; they should not need parboiling. Peel and chop the onions. Put all the ingredients in a large pan and cook gently, uncovered, for 6–8 minutes.

Drain off most of the stock if you want to serve the vegetables as a side dish; to make sure your dish is really golden, add a drop of food colouring. Alternatively, double the quantity of stock for the cooking, do not drain, and serve as a 'running' pottage.

15. Cloves were popular both for cookery and medicinal use.

Civey of Hare

SERVES SIX

*Hare yn cyve. Smyte a hare in small pecys; perboyle hem yn swete
broth with hys oun blode. Cast hym yn a cold watyr. Peke hym clene;
do hym in a pott. Clarifye the broth clene; do therto onyons & herbes
mynsyd. Take hole clovys, macys & powdyr, & drow a thyn lyour of
crustys with rede wyne. Boyle hit tyl hit be ynowghe; sesyn hit up with
powdyr of gynger, venyger & salt, & loke hit be a good colour of blod.*
(OP. 29.)

ROSEMARY

1 hare, cleaned and jointed into 6 pieces

575 ml/1 pint/2½ cups beef stock

Blood of the hare or 125 g/4 oz pig's liver, sliced

2 medium onions

1 sprig each of fresh thyme and rosemary

2 slices brown toast sprinkled with ground mixed spice

175 ml/6 fl oz/¾ cup red wine

6 parsley stalks tied in muslin with 4 whole cloves and 2 blades mace

¼ teaspoon ground ginger

Salt to taste

1 tablespoon red wine vinegar

Discard the foot joints of the hare and any flaps of skin on the saddle.
Cut through the spine between the rib-cage and fleshier saddle. Put
all the meat in a stew-pan with the stock and blood or pig's liver and
cook gently for 15 minutes. Meanwhile, peel and chop the onions
and chop the thyme and rosemary leaves; also steep the spiced toast
in the wine.

Remove the hare meat from the pan and strain the stock,
discarding the liver if used. Rinse the hare meat in cold water.
Return the stock to the pan with the chopped onions and herbs and

16. The young cook will probably need a deeper pot for the hare he is hanging, and its vegetables and wine.

add the spice bundle. Stir in the mushy soaked bread and wine. Lastly, add the meat, putting the rib-cage on top. Cover the pan and cook the civey gently for 2 hours or until the meat is tender.

Just before serving, blend the ginger and salt into the vinegar and stir them into the sauce. Discard the rib-cage. Transfer to a casserole or deep dish and serve hot.

Chicken with Rice and Almonds

SERVES SIX

Blawmanger. Tak the two del of rys, the thridde pert of almoundes;
wasch clene the rys in leuk water & turne & seth hem til thay breke &
lat it kele, and tak the melk & do it to the rys & boyle hem togedere. &
do therto whit gres & braun of hennes ground smale, and stere it wel,
and salte it & dresch it in disches. & frye almoundes in fresch gres til
they be browne, & set hem in the dissches, and strawe thereon sugre &
serue it forth. (CI. III. 28.)

225 g/8 oz long-grain rice

1.4 litres/2½ pints/6¼ cups strong chicken stock

125 g/4 oz ground almonds

450 g/1 lb poached white chicken meat, minced

2–3 tablespoons chicken fat, melted

Salt and freshly ground black pepper

GARNISH

50 g/2 oz flaked almonds, toasted

Light sprinkling of white sugar or dried saffron strands (optional)

There are several versions of this popular dish; one contains lumps of meat, another (given by the Goodman of Paris) is for invalids. I have borrowed a few details from other versions for this recipe, as I'm sure Chaucer's cook did.

Wash the rice in lukewarm water. Then boil it in 1.1 litres/2 pints/5 cups of the chicken stock until almost tender. Heat the remaining stock and use it to steep the ground almonds for about 15 minutes. Drain the rice well when done and let it cool. Then return it to the dry pan and strain in the almond 'milk'. Bring to simmering point. Stir in the chicken meat and fat, stir round and cook until the meat is heated through. Season while cooking.

17. Chaucer's cook
dressed for work,
flesh-hook in hand.

Serve the chicken and rice into warmed bowls and put a ring of toasted almond flakes around the edge of each helping. If you wish, sprinkle a very little sugar or a few saffron strands in the centre. (Saffron looks and tastes better, if affordable.)

Lombard Chicken Pasties

SERVES SIX

Chickens be set in a pasty on their backs with the breast upward and large slices of bacon on the breast, and then covered.
Item in the Lombard manner, when the chickens be plucked and prepared, take beaten eggs (to wit yolks and whites) with verjuice and spice powder and dip your chickens therein; then set them in the pasty with strips of bacon as above. (MP. Trans. E. Power.)

350 g/12 oz shortcrust or puff pastry

2 eggs, beaten

2 tablespoons verjuice or lemon juice (see page 26)

⅛ teaspoon freshly ground black pepper

½ teaspoon ground ginger

450 g/1 lb chicken or turkey breast meat, in small thin slices

3 large rashers streaky or back bacon, trimmed of fat and cut in half

No doubt the franklin in Chaucer's group who kept such a grandiose table would have served a splendid double-sized, two-crust pie at home; but small ones are better for eating on the road. In either case he would surely have told his cooks to bone the birds. Hunting for meat (or fish) bones under a pastry crust is frustrating.

Roll out the pastry and cut it into six large circles each 16 cm/6½ inches across. 'Rest' it while making the filling. Pre-heat the oven to 220°C/425°F/Gas Mark 7.

18. A pasty for an intimate supper!

Mix the beaten egg with the verjuice or lemon juice, pepper and ginger. Dip the slices of poultry meat in the mixture, then divide them between the pastry circles, placing them on one side of the round, but not right up to the edge. Lay a piece of bacon on each pile. Brush the edge of the pastry with any remaining egg mixture; if necessary, use a third egg. Fold the bare half of each pastry round over the meat and match the two pastry edges. Pinch the edges together, fluting them, or press with a fork. Prick the pastry in several places.

Bake the pasties on a baking sheet for 15 minutes. Reduce the oven temperature to 190°C/375°F/Gas Mark 5 and cook for another 20-25 minutes. Serve hot or cold.

Fig and Raisin 'Cream'

SERVES SIX

Rapey. Take half fyges and half raisouns; pike hem and waishe hem in water. Skalde hem in wyne, bray hem in a morter, and drawe hem thurgh a straynour. Cast hem in a pot and therwith powdur of peper and oother good powdours; alay it vp with flour of rys, and colour it with saundres. Salt it, seeth it & messe it forth. (Cl. IV. 85.)

125 g/4 oz well-soaked dried figs

125 g/4 oz stoned raisins

275 ml/10 fl oz/1¼ cups red wine (not too dry)

Good pinch of ground black pepper

⅓ teaspoon ground cinnamon

⅛ teaspoon ground cloves

Soft dark brown sugar to taste

3 teaspoons rice flour or cornflour

A drop or two of red food colouring

Salt to taste

Drain the figs, reserving the soaking liquid. Discard the stalk ends of the fruit and put them in a saucepan with the raisins and wine. Add the spices and a teaspoon of sugar and bring to the boil. Take off the heat and cool slightly, then turn the mixture into an electric blender and process until smooth. Add a little of the soaking water if the mixture is stubbornly solid.

Cream the rice flour or cornflour with a little more soaking water or wine and brighten the tint with a drop of food colouring. Blend the 'cream' into the dried-fruit purée. Then return the whole mixture to the saucepan and simmer until it thickens slightly. Season with salt and a little extra sugar if you wish.

The mixture can be served hot or cold over a sweet cereal dish, firm stewed fruit or – best of all – ice cream. Some versions in other manuscripts are stiffer and make a good filling for tartlets or fried puffs. One encloses the filling in pastry to make dumplings.

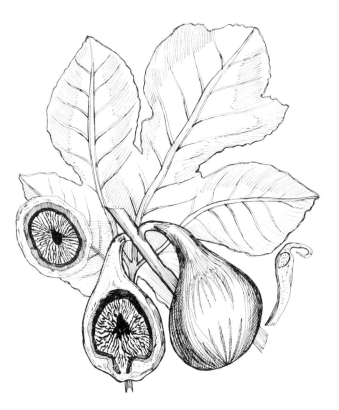

19. Figs were a favourite fruit in Lent as a spicy, sweet snack.

3

LIFE IN THE CLOISTER

Until the beginning of the thirteenth century, the diet of monks and nuns was very austere indeed. They were not allowed any animal flesh at all, and they had only one main meal a day, usually around noon, and a light supper before sundown – no breakfast and no snacks! This could be hard going when one had to get up during the night for the office of Matins followed by Lauds, then rise after a short sleep to do a morning's work before dinner.

Nor were meal times a chance for relaxation. A selected brother or sister, not perhaps a dramatic speaker, read extracts from the scriptures during meals, which one was supposed to contemplate while eating. Conversation was forbidden, so that all requests had to be made in dumb show, with some curious and often comic results.

The Church's idea for everyone was that 'fasting' was essentially a voluntary, private self-discipline, but there clearly could not be any question of opting out in a religious community. In fact, all the layman's 'fast' days and some others were observed, often including some extra deprivation such as eating barley bread instead of the household kind; while in Lent, besides the general restrictions, supper was given up completely or reduced to a snack of bread and water called (oddly, to us) a collation.

The more rigorous rules proved quite unenforcable, and were successively relaxed. Sick and aged monks had always been allowed poultry and some meat, and on a rota system a number of active monks joined them in the infirmary dining room for a few weeks every so often as a kind of holiday. Meat was allowed to the monastery's public representatives too. For instance, Church teaching required that monks should shelter and feed all who came to their door with the best they could offer; that was why the abbot or prior in charge could accept and use the standard gifts of hunted game from laymen. However, when a public display of holiness was called for, as at a royal or similar feast, an alternative fish menu as sumptuous as the meat one was provided for clerics (and anyone else who might be undergoing a private fast on that day).

Even the less rigorous restrictions became mellowed with time. The collation could become a snack of delicious spiced toasts and other titbits, such as candied and dried fruits, if the monastery could afford them. Candied fruits were often quite plentiful because any sizable monastery kept beehives and, like the Goodman of Paris, used its own honey for preserving; the bees' main function in a monastery being to supply wax for the church candles. (Bees were

21. A cheerful cellarer.

20. Retribution for monkish misdeeds!

believed to be holy and virginal and able to whisper in God's ear, so only beeswax would do for light in God's house.)

Relaxed though the restrictions might be, many and varied ways were found by wilier brothers and sisters to get round those which remained. Visiting bishops found almost continuous cases of gluttonous living about which to complain. Some roistering monks and frivolous nuns simply ignored altogether the rules which did not suit them, and gave a bad name to those who were too good (or too poor) to contravene them. Chaucer's jovial monk in *The Canterbury Tales* was probably not far from a real-life model.

CINQUEFOIL

Barley Bread

MAKES 2 × 600 g/1¼ LB LOAVES

Monks and nuns were not, as a rule, supposed to eat fine white bread
(see page 37). Household or barley bread was deemed more sustaining
for people who spent long hours in toil or prayer. Barley was always
available where monks brewed ale. This recipe is based on what I have
been able to learn from various manuscripts about traditional early
English bread-making.

500 g/1 lb 2 oz strong wholemeal flour

225 g/8 oz barley flour

25 g/1 oz rice flour

½ tablespoon salt

15 g/½oz fresh yeast

60 ml/2½ fl oz/⅓ cup brown ale

about 425 ml/15 fl oz/2 cups warm water

2 teaspoons clear honey

Mix the dry ingredients in a warmed bowl. Blend the yeast to a cream
with a little ale, then mix with 350 ml/12 fl oz/1½ cups of the water
and the honey. Stir the mixture into the dry goods and mix to a firm
dough, adding extra water as needed. Knead until the dough feels
elastic. Shape it into a ball. Lift it out of the bowl and oil the inside of
the bowl lightly. Return the dough, cover it loosely with oiled
polythene and leave the bowl in a warm place until the dough has
almost doubled in bulk. Punch it down, then shape it into two equal-
sized oblong or round loaves. Place in two bread or deep cake tins.
(For traditional round loaves, use deep cake tins with removable
bases.). Make a cross-cut in the centre of round loaves. Pre-heat the
oven to 230°C/450°F/Gas Mark 8.

Cover the dough lightly with a cloth and leave in a warm place
until well risen. Bake the loaves for 20–25 minutes; they should

sound hollow when turned out and tapped underneath. If they need a few minutes longer, cover them lightly with greased foil and lower the oven heat slightly. Cool them under a cloth, on a wire rack. Do not cut until quite cold.

Leeks and Sops in Wine
SERVES SIX

Slyt soppes. Take white of lekes and slyt hem, and do hem to seeth in wyne, oile and salt. Tost brede and lay in disshes, and cast the sewe aboue, and serue it forth. (Cl. IV. 82.)

8–12 leeks, depending on size

2 tablespoons olive oil

Sprinkling of salt

1 bottle (75 cl) white wine

3–4 slices soft-grain white bread, freshly toasted

Even if Chaucer's franklin did not eat leeks for breakfast, he would have found this classy version of 'sops in wine' a treat. Monks certainly did, especially in Lent when they often had only bread sops and water for supper – officially. Although simple, this was not a poor man's dish. Poor people used whole leeks, and could not afford white wine when broth was forbidden. Olive oil and white bread (mentioned in another recipe very like this one) were luxuries too.

Slice the white parts of the leeks thinly. (Keep the rest for everyday pottage.) Simmer the sliced leeks, oil and salt in the wine until the leek slices are soft. Meanwhile, break or cut the toast into small pieces and divide them between six soup bowls. Cover them with the leek slices and hot wine. Serve as soon as the toast sops have softened.

22. A baker who gave short weight might be dragged through the streets on a sledge with the offending loaf round his (or her) neck.

Pike in Galentyne

SERVES SIX

23. A stylised drawing of a noble couple and retainers having a 'fysshe' day meal.

Auter pike in Galentyne. Take browne brede, and stepe it in a quarte of vinegre, and a pece of wyne for a pike, and quarteren of pouder canell, and drawe it thorgh a streynour skilfully thik, and cast it in a potte, and lete boyle; and cast there-to pouder peper, or ginger, or of clowes, and lete kele. And then take a pike, and seth him in good sauce, and take him vp, and lete him kele a litul; and ley him in a boll for to cary him yn; and cast the sauce vnder him and aboue him, that he be al y-hidde in the sauce; and cary him whether euer thou wolt.
(Harl. 4016. p. 101.)

About 1.4 kg/3 lb middle cut of pike or similar large fish

275 ml/10 fl oz/1¼ cups white wine

2 tablespoons white wine vinegar

2–3 parsley stalks

Salt

3 slices brown bread, crusts removed

¼ teaspoon ground cinnamon

⅛ teaspoon ground white pepper

125 g/4 oz onions, peeled and chopped

Oil for frying

Gelatine (optional)

Put the fish in a pan, add the wine, vinegar, parsley stalks and enough salted water to cover the fish and poach gently for 15 minutes. Turn off the heat; if necessary, the fish will finish cooking in the liquid as it cools. Cover the pan and cool to tepid before finishing the dish.

Carefully lift the fish out of the pan. Reserve the cooking liquid. Put the bread in a bowl and add enough of the liquid to cover it.

Skin the fish and take out the spine and other bones; pike has a line of thin bones through the middle of the body flesh on each side.

24. Pike, the lazy predator, makes firm-fleshed eating.

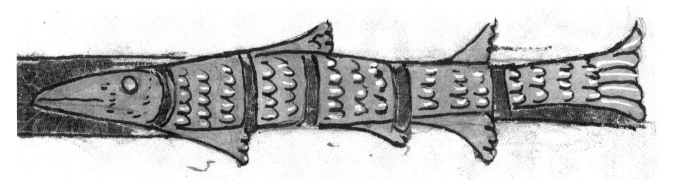

59

Cut all the flesh into small pieces both to get at them and to make a manageable dish.

Strain the remaining cooking liquid into a clean pan. Put 425 ml/15 fl oz/2 cups of it into an electric blender with the soaked bread, cinnamon and pepper; process until smooth. Return the mixture to the liquid in the pan. Fry the onions in a little oil until soft, and add them to the liquid too. Taste for seasoning, add the pieces of fish and re-heat gently to serve.

If you want a cold dish, keep the fish pieces and fried onions aside while you measure and taste the liquid, then re-heat it with enough gelatine to stiffen it; if you had cooked a whole fish, it would have jellied without help. Add the fish pieces and onions, turn into a mould and leave to set in the refrigerator.

Haddock in Tasty Sauce

SERVES SIX

Haddoke in Cyuee. Shal be yopened & ywasshe clene & ysode & yrosted on a gridel; grind peper & saffron, bred and ale mynce oynons, fri hem in ale, and do therto, and salt: boille hit, do thyn haddok in plateres, and the ciuey aboue, and ghif forth. (Laud 533. p.114.)

900 g/2 lb haddock fillet

Salt

75 g/3 oz onions, peeled and finely chopped

Oil or butter for frying

¼ teaspoon ground white pepper

75 g/3 oz fine soft white breadcrumbs

125 ml/4 fl oz/½ cup brown ale

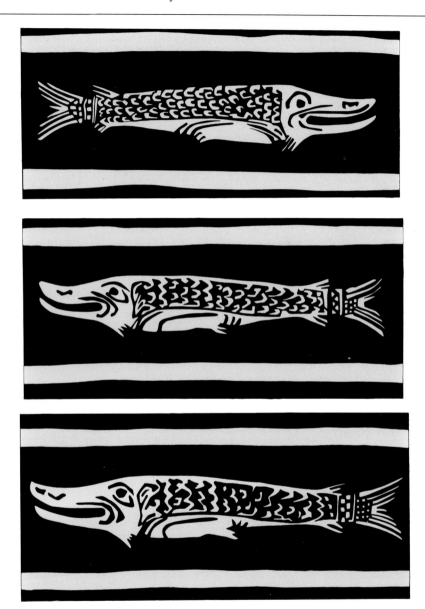

25. Fish floor tiles at Westminster Abbey, perhaps to remind
the monks of fasting and penitence.

A *civet* is a piquant stew, usually made with meat of furred game; hence the brown ale. In old dishes the cook is usually told to 'drawe' a fish, animal or bird when it is merely to be cleaned, so I have interpreted *yopened* to mean that the creature was split right open and boned. It could then easily be cut in pieces as in a *civet*, and eaten with a spoon. Oil could be used by strict (and wealthy) dieters for frying food in Lent, but poor folks would probably use butter, and omit the costly saffron as I have done – the ale kills its colour anyway.

Skin the haddock fillet and cut it into several pieces. Put enough salted water into a shallow pan to cover the fish and bring it to the boil. Put in the fish and simmer for a moment or two, then cover the pan and draw it off the heat; the fish will continue to cook in the hot water while you make the sauce. For this, fry the onions in the fat until just beginning to brown. Mix the pepper with the breadcrumbs and add them to the onions with the ale and 225 ml/8 fl oz of the water used to cook the fish. Process until smooth in an electric blender, then simmer for a few minutes to reheat.

While simmering, drain the remaining water from the cooked fish and put the pieces on the grill rack. Brush them with a little melted fat, then place them under a hot grilling flame until they are just beginning to glaze. Cut them into bite-sized or serving portions and spoon some sauce over them. Serve the rest separately. If you do not like ale or beer use cider instead.

Jowtes with Almond Milk

SERVES SIX

Iowtes of almaund mylke. Take erbes; boile hem, hewe hem, and
grynde hem smale. Take almaundus iblaunchede; grynde hem and
drawe hem vp with water. Set hem on the fire and seeth the iowtes with
the mylke, and cast thereon sugur & salt, & serue it forth.
(CI. IV. 89.)

900 g/2 lb spinach

125 g/4 oz inner green part of leeks (see method)

2 tablespoons chopped fresh herbs (e.g. chives
or Welsh onion, thyme and hyssop)

1.1 litres/2 pints/5 cups water

125 g/4 oz ground almonds

15 g/½ oz rice flour or cornflour

Salt and pepper

Pinch of sugar

Pinch of grated nutmeg or grated lemon rind (optional)

This filling soup is a rich dark green when prepared with winter leaves. It probably made an entire meal for the brothers when on their Lenten diet.

Prepare the spinach by taking off the stalks and washing the leaves thoroughly; it should weigh about 700 g/1½ lb when prepared. Strip the green ends of the leeks to expose the tightly folded green part at the top of the white stem; slice it across thinly. Strip the herb leaves off their stems and chop them. Put all the greens and herbs into a large stewpan and add 1.1 litres/2 pints/5 cups water. Bring to simmering point, cover and cook gently until the leek slices are just tender.

Put the ground almonds and flour in a saucepan. Add enough cold water to make a smooth cream.

HYSSOP

63

Drain the spinach, reserving the cooking liquid. Chop and purée most of the spinach in a food processor, keeping a few whole leaves for garnishing. Stir in the almond 'milk' and about half the reserved spinach liquid; add the flavourings. Return the mixture to the pan and simmer, stirring, until well heated through and slightly thickened. Add extra liquid if you wish; serve in a tureen with the garnishing leaves on top.

THYME

Almond Milk

Vurst nim of alemauns, & hwyte of heom one pertie, ah hwyte summe hole & the other do to grinden. Sothen nim the hole alemauns & corf heom to quartes; sothen nim fat broth & swete of porc other of vthur vlehs; tempre thin alemauns & sothen drauh out thi milke & sothe do hit in an veyre crouhe . . . (Cl. I. 56.)

Ground almonds

Water, stock, wine or other liquid

Rice flour or cornflour

Salt

You can make thin or thick almond milk, as suits your dish, by adapting the quantity of almonds to the amount of liquid in your recipe. In either case your object is to produce a liquid or purée as smooth as possible. The method is the same.

First pulverise the almonds in a blender (not a food processor) or in a coffee or nut mill. Put them in a bowl and pour on enough boiling liquid to make a smooth cream. Leave to stand for 10–15 minutes, then rub the mixture through a metal sieve.

This mixture may be smooth enough. If not, cream a little rice flour or cornflour with it and heat until it thickens slightly. Then add any extra liquid the recipe calls for, and a scrap of salt.

I find that 125 g/4 oz almonds and 1 tablespoon rice flour moistened with 275 ml/10 fl oz/1¼ cups liquid produces a 'milk' suitable for most purposes.

Almond milk might be used whenever a flavoured liquid base without meat products, cow's milk, cream or eggs was needed. It could also be used as a thickener – or just for its aroma and flavour.

26. Almonds – an essential ingredient in medieval menus, except for the poorest.

Fried Fig Pastries

SERVES SIX

Tourteletes in Frytour. Take figus & grynde hem smal; do therin saffron & powdur fort. Close hem in foyles of dowe, & frye hem in oyle. Clarifye hony & flamme hem therwyt; ete hem hote or colde.
(CI. IV. 157.)

450 g/1 lb dried figs, soaked, drained and minced
(reserve the soaking liquid)

Powder fort mixture made with ⅛ teaspoon each ground
ginger and cloves, pinch of black pepper

¼ teaspoon dried saffron strands moistened with fig soaking liquid

¼ teaspoon salt

1 egg, separated, and 1 egg white

6–7 sheets filo or strudel pastry

Oil for frying

About 225 ml/8 fl oz/1 cup warmed clear honey (optional)

Apothecaries made up and sold a number of spice mixtures ready for use. There were no set recipes for these mixtures, so each practitioner could suit his own taste; but the general style and strength of the 'mix' was reflected by its name. Powder fort almost always contained black pepper, ginger, cloves or cumin and other strong spices. Powder douce (see page 92) contained milder, sweeter spices such as cinnamon and sugar.

Figs were eaten all through Lent but particularly in the week before Easter to commemorate Christ's last ride into Jerusalem. They were a special treat for monks and nuns.

In a food processor combine the minced figs, spices and saffron, salt and egg yolk.

Beat the egg whites until liquid. Lightly brush the top sheet of pastry with egg white. Mark the short side of the pastry sheet at 7.5-

27. An apothecary's shop, where spice mixtures were sold.

cm/3-inch intervals. Then cut the sheet into strips 7.5 cm/3 inches wide. Put a dab of fig mixture on the end of one sheet and roll the strip up like a mini-Swiss roll. Pinch the ends to seal in the fig mixture.

Repeat this process until you have used all the fig mixture; remember to brush every pastry sheet with egg white before cutting it into strips.

Fry the rolls, a few at a time, in deep or shallow oil as you prefer. Serve them with warmed honey spooned over if you like a very sweet sauce. (The old recipe tells you to baste the rolls with the honey, so you may be meant to finish processing the rolls like Crêpes Suzette.)

4

THE GOODMAN
OF PARIS

The upright French landowner of sixty whose recipes fill this section is revealed to us in Eileen Power's translation of his book as one of the most prepossessing characters of his time. This is partly because he is not a public figure whose words and actions are displayed for praise or blame by a biographer, nor is he writing for money; as far as we can tell, he is genuinely composing, from various sources and his own experience, a housewife's manual just for the use of his fifteen-year-old bride.

This age gap between husband and wife was not unusual in the late fourteenth century. Disease and violence, and for women frequent unhygienic child-births, took their toll, so most people of reasonable means could expect to marry at least twice; and it may have been no bad thing for a prosperous man to take on a young girl to care for him in old age, with a guarantee that he would leave her well provided for and capable of handling a sizable establishment. The Goodman, who seems to have been some kind of civil servant or official, was such a man; he had a farm in the country as well as his house in Paris, and he appears to have been on speaking terms with members of the nobility, or so he implies.

The first part of his book is a manual of moral behaviour and deportment which repeats the precepts and the usual exemplary stories of the day; Chaucer did the same in *The Canterbury Tales*. Indeed these two books, written at the same time by two mature men

28. The young St Barbara in this picture might well have been the Goodman's girl-wife asserting her views.

of the same social class, are excellent glosses on each other. But the Goodman, instead of relying on ironical description and tales, prudish or coarse, as Chaucer did, provides his girl-wife with practical instructions. He details how to handle servants and tradesmen, including the farm labourers on his estate; and how to cope with the garden and to use its products, with lists of plants for different purposes. He also describes grand dinners and suppers (to be admired but not copied) and explains how to shop in the Paris markets for pre-prepared 'goodies' – for white breads and wafers, spice mixtures and ready-made sauces. Not content with this, he provides a detailed and remarkably modern collection of recipes copied from other books in his library.

In these recipes he features, first, thin and thickened pottages – that is, pot-boiled foods – many of them plain vegetable dishes, others complex and colourful. But he gives due attention to fresh-water and sea fish, to butcher's meats, poultry and game, to fruit mixtures for Lent, and to flans, jellies, rissoles and pancakes. He has a section, too, on pottages and beverages for the sick, and another on preserves of nuts, vegetables and orange peel, which could be candied in honey from St John's Day (nuts) to All Saints' Day (turnips and carrots).

He can be superstitious, our Goodman, and a scrap pompous at times. But his sturdy commonsense shows in his shrewd suggestions for small kitchen economies; and his directions to his wife for the care of her maids, her livestock and even wild birds are wise and humane.

Overall, he gives us the most vivid and valuable commentary on the domestic life and folk at the end of the fourteenth century which we could hope to find.

29. A typical
medieval market.

Cabbage Chowder

SERVES SIX

Caboches in potage. Take caboches and quarter hem, and seeth hem in gode broth with oynouns ymynced and the whyte of lekes yslyt and ycorue smale. And do therto safroun & salt, and force it with powdour douce. (Cl. IV. 6.)

600 g/1 ¼ lb firm-hearted cabbage or 700 g/1 ½ lb
open-hearted cabbage or spring greens

225 g/8 oz onions, peeled and finely chopped

225 g/8 oz white part of leeks, thinly sliced into rings

⅛ teaspoon dried saffron strands

½ teaspoon salt

¼ teaspoon each ground coriander, cinnamon and sugar

850 ml/1 ½ pints/3 ¾ cups chicken or vegetable stock

The Goodman of Paris had quite a lot to say about cabbages, from the small spring sprouts for salads to the frostbitten winter leaves; only his recommendation to boil cabbages all morning is best ignored when using modern vegetables.

CORIANDER

30. Assorted herbs being selected for kitchen use.

If using a firm-hearted cabbage cut it into eight segments, and remove the centre core. If using an open-hearted cabbage or greens, cut off the stalks and cut the leaves into strips. Put into a large pan with the prepared onions and leeks. Stir the saffron, salt and spices into the stock, adjusting the quantity of salt if required, then pour the mixture over the vegetables. Cook gently, covered, for about 20 minutes or until segments of firm cabbage are tender.

This will make a main-course soup for supper if you add sippets of toast and small strips of fried bacon – both well-known medieval additions.

'Departed' Creamed Fish

SERVES SIX AS A STARTER

To make mortreux of fisch. Tak plays or fresch meluel or merlyng &
seth it in fayre water, and then tak awey the skyn & the bones & presse
the fisch in a cloth & bray it in a mortere, and tempre it vp with
almond melk, & bray poudere of gynger & sugre togedere & departe
the mortreux on tweyne in two pottes & coloure that on with saffroun
& dresch it in disches, half of that on & half of that other, & strawe
poudere of gyngere & sugre on that on & clene sugre on that other &
serue it forth. (CI. III. 26.)

600 g/1¼ lb skinned cod fillet

Sea salt

125 g/4 oz ground almonds

2 teaspoons rice flour or cornflour

3 tablespoons deep yellow saffron water or food colouring

½ teaspoon ground ginger

¾ teaspoon white sugar

The 'standing' (thick) pottage or pâté called *mortrews* could contain
either fish or meat. Its thickening made it a better-than-usual dish,
even without extra colour. 'Departed', as it sounds, just means that
the dish is 'parted in two', that is, bi-coloured. The Goodman
suggested a chicken liver or meat *mortrews*, but I think his young wife
would have clapped her hands over this one on 'fysshe dayes'.

To make it, poach the fish fillet in about 575 ml/1 pint/2½ cups of
salted water until cooked through. Drain off the cooking liquid into a
measuring jug. Pour 275 ml/10 fl oz/1¼ cups of the hot measured
liquid over the almonds in a bowl.

Press the fish under a cloth or kitchen paper to squeeze out excess
moisture, then flake it. Strain the almond 'milk' into a jug, stirring to
separate the free liquid from the almond sludge in the strainer. Put

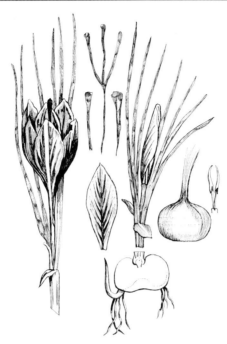

31. The most admired finishing touch to any dish was the luxurious golden tint of saffron.

the liquid into the goblet of an electric blender, followed by the flaked fish, and process until smooth. If the mixture is too stiff to process easily, add a little more fish cooking liquid. Turn the mixture into a bowl.

In a small saucepan, cream the rice flour or cornflour with 3 or 4 tablespoons of fish cooking liquid, then heat the mixture gently until it thickens. Stir this 'cream' into the fish mixture and season with salt.

Put half the mixture into a separate bowl and tint it deep gold with the saffron water or food colouring. Combine the ground ginger and ¼ teaspoon of the sugar and mix into the golden fish, reserving a little of the mixture for sprinkling. If you like ginger, increase the quantity.

Serve the *mortrews* in six scallop shells or small saucers, putting a coloured and a plain spoonful of mixture side by side in each. Chill until needed. Just before serving, sprinkle the remaining ginger/sugar mix on the gold portions and the remaining ½ teaspoon plain sugar on the white portions.

Capon or Chicken Crowned with Eggs

SERVES SIX

Capouns in councy. Take capouns and rost hem right hoot, that they be not half ynough, and hewe hem to gobbettes, and cast hem in a pot; do therto clene broth. Seeth hem that they be tendre. Take brede and the self broth and draw it up yfere; take strong powdour and safroun and salt and cast therto. Take ayren and seeth hem harde; take out the yolkes and hew the whyte, take the pot fro the fyre and cast the whyte therinne. Messe the dysshes therwith, and lay the yolkes aboue hool and flour it with clowes. (Cl. IV. 24.)

1 × 2.3–2.7 kg/5–6 lb capon or large roasting chicken

chicken fat or butter for greasing

850 ml/1½ pints/3¾ cups chicken stock

¼ teaspoon dried saffron strands

125 g/4 oz soft-grain white breadcrumbs

Sea salt to taste

¼–½ teaspoon each ground black pepper, cinnamon and ginger

⅛ teaspoon ground cloves

6 eggs, hard-boiled

The Goodman said stoutly that stuffing and tinting chickens was too difficult for a commoner's cook. Perhaps he decided this dish was easier.

Pre-heat the oven to 220°C/425°F/Gas Mark 7. Grease the breast of the bird with fat and roast it for 15–20 minutes or until browned. Cool it slightly, then cut the flesh off the bones, removing the skin if you wish. Cut the meat into bite-sized pieces. Put them in a pan with the stock, cover the pan and cook gently for 25 minutes or until the meat is cooked. While cooking transfer 3 or 4 tablespoons of stock to a bowl and steep the saffron in it.

Strain the stock from the cooked chicken into a clean pan and add

32. The young girl feeds the chickens on the well-appointed farm.

the saffron-tinted stock. Keep the meat warm in a covered dish while you make the sauce. Mix the breadcrumbs with the salt and ground spices, then stir the mixture into the stock. Simmer it for a few minutes, stirring it occasionally to make a thickened sauce.

Separate the egg yolks and whites without breaking the yolks. Chop the whites finely. Mix the chicken meat into the hot sauce and turn it on to a warmed serving platter. Edge the dish with chopped egg white and crown it with the whole golden yolks.

CLOVE PINK

Cherry Pottage

SERVES SIX

Syrosye. Tak cheryes & do out the stones & grynde hem wel & draw hem thorw a streynour & do it in a pot. & do therto whit gres or swete botere & myed wastel bred, & cast therto good wyn & sugre, & salte it & stere it wel togedere, & dresse it in disches; and set theryn clowe gilofre, & strewe sugre aboue. (CI. III. 33.)

900 g/2 lb fresh ripe red cherries

350 ml/12 fl oz/1 ½ cups red wine

175 g/6 oz white sugar

50 g/2 oz unsalted butter

225 g/8 oz soft white breadcrumbs

Pinch of salt

Flower heads of small clove pinks or gilded whole cloves
(according to season)

Coarse white sugar for sprinkling

This cherry pottage was a genteel dish, being made with wine and white bread, so it merited the use of precious white sugar. Soluble gold gouache can be used to gild the tops of whole cloves, but do not bite on them; they stun the taste-buds.

Wash the cherries and discard the stems and stones. Purée the fruit in a blender with 150 ml/5 fl oz/10 tablespoons of the wine and half the sugar. Add a little more wine if you need to. Melt the butter in a saucepan and add the fruit purée, breadcrumbs, remaining wine and sugar, and the salt. Simmer, stirring steadily, until the purée is very thick. Pour into a serving bowl, cover and leave to cool. When quite cold, decorate the edge of the bowl with flowers or whole cloves, and sprinkle coarse sugar over the centre.

Any young hostess, married or not, would enjoy showing off this pretty dish.

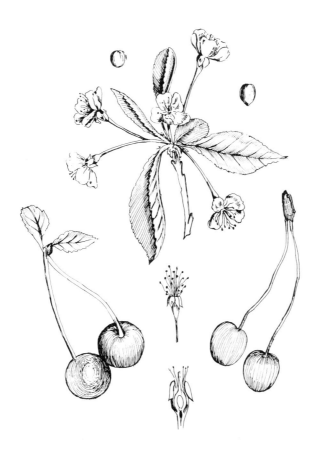

33. Black and red cherries grew wild in plenty.

Mixed Pickles

MAKES 2.3 kg/5 lb

Compost. Take rote of persel, of pasternak, of rafens, scrape hem and waische him clene. Take rapes & caboches, ypared and ycorue. Take an erthen panne with clene water & set it on the fire; cast all thise therinne. Whan they buth boiled cast therto peeres & perboile hem wel. Take alle thise thynges vp & lat it kele on a faire cloth. Do therto salt; whan it is colde, do hit in a vessel; take vyneger & powdour & safroun & do therto, & lat alle thise thynges lye therein al night, other al day. Take wyne greke & hony clarified togider; take lumbarde mustard & raisouns coraunce, al hoole, & grynde powdour of canel, powdour douce & aneys hole, & fenell seed. Take alle thise thynges & cast togyder in a pot of erthe, & take thereof whan thou wilt & serue forth. (CI. IV. 103.)

900 g/2 lb mixed parsley roots, carrots, radishes and turnips

450 g/1 lb white cabbage

450 g/1 lb hard eating pears

6 tablespoons salt

1 teaspoon ground ginger

½ teaspoon dried saffron strands

425 ml/15 fl oz/2 cups white wine vinegar

50 g/2 oz currants

575 ml/1 pint/2½ cups fruity white wine

6 tablespoons clear honey

1 teaspoon French mustard

⅛ teaspoon each ground cinnamon and black pepper

¼ teaspoon each anise and fennel seeds

50 g/2 oz white sugar

34. The housekeeper teaches her pupil to care for wines, as well as how to use them in making preserves.

The Goodman had recipes for pickling walnuts and various vegetables and fruits grown on his farm separately, but he soaked the whole lot in honey – to the ruin of his household's teeth, I should think! This recipe is much more like the modern ones.

Prepare the root vegetables and slice them thinly. Core and shred the cabbage. Put these vegetables into a large pan of water and bring slowly to the boil. Peel, core and cut up the pears and add them to the pan. Cook until they start to soften. Drain the contents of the pan and spread in a 5-cm/2-inch layer in a shallow non-metallic dish.

Sprinkle with the salt, ginger, saffron and 4 tablespoons of the vinegar. Leave, covered, for 12 hours. Rinse well, then add the currants. Pack into sterilised storage jars, with at least 2.5 cm/1 inch headspace.

Put the wine and honey in a pan. Bring to simmering point and skim. Add the rest of the vinegar and all the remaining spices and sugar. Reduce the heat and stir without boiling until the sugar dissolves. Bring back to the boil. Pour over the vegetables, covering them with 1 cm/½ inch liquid. Cover with vinegar-proof seals and store.

Mushroom Pasties

SERVES SIX

Mushrooms of one night are the best, if they are small, red inside, and closed at the top: and they should be peeled and then washed in hot water and parboiled, and if you wish to put them in a pasty add oil, cheese and spice powder. (MP. Trans. E. Power.)

450 g/1 lb home-made or bought shortcrust pastry, thawed if frozen

450 g/1 lb button mushrooms

Salt

2 tablespoons olive oil

50 g/2 oz Cheddar cheese, grated

½ teaspoon salt

⅛ teaspoon freshly ground black pepper

¼ teaspoon dry mustard powder

1 egg, beaten

Use two-thirds of the pastry to line small, deep pans. Chill while making the filling. Pre-heat the oven to 200°C/400°F/Gas Mark 6.

Trim off the bottoms of the mushroom stems; then dip the mushrooms in boiling salted water, holding them in a sieve. Drain them, pat dry, then chop or slice them. Put them in a bowl and mix them with the oil, cheese and seasonings. Fill the mixture into the pastry cases. Roll out the remaining pastry and use it to make lids for the pasties. Seal the lids with beaten egg. Decorate the tops with pastry trimmings and brush with the remaining egg. Make a small cross-cut in the centre of each lid.

Bake the little pies in the oven for 15–18 minutes. Serve warm.

At home, no doubt, the Goodman, who kept a well-furnished table, would serve a large double-crust pasty or plate pie – but on his journeys to and from the farm, small ones probably seemed more suitable. Make a 23-cm/9-inch plate pie if you prefer.

35. 'Mushrooms of one night are the best'.

5

OF MANNERS
AND MEALS

In the later Middle Ages, children of good birth were often sent
away from home to be educated even before they reached their
teens. Those who would one day manage large estates were taken
into the household of a great magnate or Church dignitary where
formal meals, service and manners were the daily routine (which
might not be the case at home).

Under the skilled teaching of John Russell, Duke Humphrey of
Gloucester's Marshal, for instance, squires-to-be learned the entire
care of the person of a 'lord' from morning till night: how he should
be bathed, dressed, attended at meals and served. Carving was an art
to be learned as much as sword-play, and good manners at table were
essential when everyone at the tables of lower status in the hall
shared a plate and a helping with another – his messmate. Not least,
the 'young gentlemen' received detailed instruction on menu planning, table-laying and also on diet, as in this verse:

> Butter is a wholesome food, first and last[1]
> for it soothes the stomach and helps one to
>   get rid of poisons
> also it helps a man as an aperient and so gets
>   rid of ill humours
> and with white bread, it has a lingering flavour.

36. A lecture on
health.

Milk, cream, curds and also rose junket,
   they close a man's stomach and so are binding;
you must eat hard cheese[2] after them if you sup late
   and drink resinated wine to guard against constipation.

1. Either, 'in youth and age' or 'at morning and evening'.
2. Some authorities took the opposite view, that hard cheese 'closed
   the stomach'.

37. Younger boys got time-honoured discipline.

This education, by making the young sprigs of nobility the servants of princes, equipped them well for their future lives; they learned not only courtesy and hostmanship but also estate management and how to handle staff, which they would one day need to do on their own account. It is the type of medieval education we know best because it has been scrupulously documented in the manuscript collection published as *The Babees Book*. But it was not the only type for children of affluent parents. Boys and girls who stayed at home had tutors or governesses, and there were boarding schools, usually in religious houses. Lads whose parents had 'given' them to the Church or who could not keep them at home for some reason were sometimes brought up by monks until old enough to decide whether they had a vocation. If they decided to enter the Church, they might finish their education at Oxford University.

Girls without means might occasionally be trained by nuns, perhaps as working lay sisters. But most boarding-school girls were wealthy orphans who were 'put into care' by their guardians to protect them, and to train them in the courtesies and housekeeping befitting a gentlewoman.

At home, well-bred girls had to know at least as much as boys about the social status of different foods when the household dined together; who should get what and how much. They had to know when fish must be served, the etiquette of giving alms from the table, and the whole business of domestic preserving, whether of foods and drinks or herbs and medicines. Boys learned the more showy tasks such as displaying their skill in carving and their diet sense in ending the meal with cheese if they had a choice.

Green Pea Pottage

SERVES SIX

Perrey of pesoun. Take pesoun and seeth hem fast, and couere hem, til thei berst; thenne take hem vp and cole hem thurgh a cloth. Take oynouns and mynce hem, and seeth hem in the same sewe, and oile therwith; cast therto sugur, salt, and safroun, and seeth hem wel therafter, and serue hem forth. (CI. IV. 71.)

1.1 litres/2 pints/5 cups water

700 g/1½ lb garden peas, shelled

350 g/12 oz onions, peeled and finely chopped

1½ tablespoons oil

¼ teaspoon pulverised dried saffron strands, steeped
in 4 tablespoons boiling water (optional)

1–1½ teaspoons soft light brown sugar

1 teaspoon sea salt or to taste

This vegetable purée was probably most often served in Lent when the last dried white peas of the winter store were being used; this is a fair guess because onions were used to flavour and saffron to colour the dish. However, it could also be made in summer, using fresh green peas, although more floury than ours. (Using modern green peas, the saffron can be omitted.)

Bring the water to the boil and tip in the peas. Add the chopped onions and the soaked saffron if used. Cook gently until the peas are quite soft. Sieve both the liquid and solids into a clean pan, or purée them together in batches in an electric blender. Return the purée to the pan, and simmer for 6–7 minutes or until the soup is the consistency you want; season before serving. Remember that, in the Middle Ages, the thicker a purée was, the better its quality was thought to be.

38. In medieval pictures even the Apostles had their pottage served at the dressour (serving table).

Braised Beef

SERVES SIX

Stwed Beeff. Take faire Ribbes of ffresh beef, And (if thou wilt) roste hit til hit be nygh ynowe; then put hit in a faire possenet; caste ther-to parcely and oynons mynced, reysons of corauns, powder peper, canel, clowes, saundres, safferon, and salt; then caste there-to wyn and a litull vynegre; sette a lyd on the potte, and let hit boile sokingly on a fair charcole til hit be ynogh; then lay the fflesh, in disshes, and the sirippe there-vppon, And serve it forth. (Harl. 4016. p.72.)

900 g/2 lb boned and rolled beef ribs (braising joint)

Dripping or other fat for roasting

2 tablespoons chopped parsley

2 medium onions, peeled and chopped

2 tablespoons currants

1 teaspoon whole black peppercorns

½ teaspoon ground cinnamon

¼ teaspoon ground cloves

3–4 juniper berries or 2 fresh bay leaves

Pinch of pulverised dried saffron strands (optional)

1 teaspoon sea salt

275 ml/10 fl oz/1¼ cups red wine

2 teaspoons red wine vinegar

This was a suitable carving joint for a beginner to tackle.

Pre-heat the oven to 190°C/375°F/Gas Mark 5. Smear the beef with the fat and roast it on a rack for 40 minutes. Transfer it with its drippings to a flameproof casserole or stewpan. Cover it with the parsley, onions, currants, spices and salt, and add the wine and vinegar at the side of the pan. Cover and cook gently for 45 minutes on top of the stove or at 160°C/325°F/Gas Mark 3 in the oven for the same time. Remove to a board for carving. Strain the wine and juices in the pan, and dribble a little 'sauce' over each helping.

39. A trainee carver presents a dish of sliced meat for approval.

Lasagne Layered with Cheese
SERVES SIX

Losyns. Take good broth and do in an erthen pot. Take flour of paynedemayn and make therof past with water, and make therof thynne foyles as paper with a roller; drye it harde and seeth it in broth. Take chese ruayn grated and lay it in disshes with powdour douce, and lay theron loseyns isode as hoole as thou myght, and above powdour and chese; and so twyse or thryse, & serue it forth. (CI. IV. 50.)

9–10 sheets lasagne (broad noodles) made with white flour

1.7 litres/3 pints/7½ cups meat or chicken stock or water

Butter for greasing

Ground mace and cardamom or cinnamon
and a little white pepper for spicing

About 175 g/6 oz full-fat hard cheese (such as Cheddar), grated

This would have been thought (by some) an ideal dish as a last course, to 'seal in' the alcohol so often imbibed too freely by the young. You can, if you wish, prepare your own lasagne as the medieval cooks did. But commercially produced dried pasta makes an equally simple and comforting dish for meatless meals.

Choose a square or oblong baking dish which will hold the pasta in three layers. If you pile it higher in a smaller dish, it may be difficult to slice and serve six helpings.

Bring the stock or water to the boil in a fairly big pan and boil the lasagne in three or four batches until all the sheets are cooked. As each batch is done, remove the sheets with tongs or a pair of forks to a warmed, damp tea-towel on a flat work-top and lay them flat side by side.

Grease the inside of your chosen dish with butter. Sprinkle the bottom lightly with spices and a quarter of the cheese. Cover with a layer of pasta, trimmed to fit the dish if required. Repeat the layers of spice, cheese and pasta twice, and end with a last layer of spice and cheese. Re-heat until the cheese is melted.

40. A young squire buying cheese.

Pork Rolls

SERVES SIX (ABOUT 24 SNACKS)

Tartlettes. Take pork ysode and grynde it small with safronn, medle it
with ayren and raisons of coraunce, and powdor fort, and salt; and
make a foile of dowhg and close the fars thereinne. Cast the tartlettes in
a pan with faire water boillyng and salt, take of the clene flesh without
ayren, and boile it in gode broth. Cast thereto powdor-douce and salt,
and messe the tartletes in disches, and helde the sewe theronne.
(FC. Antiq. Cul. 50.)

700 g/1½ lb lean cooked pork without skin or bone

½ teaspoon salt

40 g/1½ oz currants

Powder fort mixture made with ⅓ teaspoon ground cumin;
⅛ teaspoon each ground black pepper and ground ginger

1 egg, separated, and 1 egg white

6–8 sheets filo or strudel pastry

SAUCE

575 ml/1 pint/2½ cups strong chicken stock

Powder douce mixture made with ⅛ teaspoon ground coriander;
pinch each of ground cinnamon and brown sugar or to taste

Mince the pork and set 225 g/8 oz aside. Put the remaining 450 g/1 lb
in a bowl and add the salt, currants and powder fort mixture. Beat the
egg yolk and use it to bind the mixture.

Stack the pastry sheets in a pile, making sure that they separate
easily. They are usually 45–50 cm/18–20 inches long. Beat the egg
whites and use to brush the top sheet of pastry lightly. Starting from
one short side, cut it into long strips 7.5 cm/3 inches wide. Place a
small teaspoon of the pork mixture on the end of one strip and roll
the pastry up like a Swiss roll. Press the ends to seal in the meat.

41. Pouring the wine and water to go with spicy snacks.

Repeat this procedure, using the other top sheet strips, then brush the next sheet and continue rolling up the mini-rolls until all the mixture is used.

Drop the rolls, a few at a time, into gently boiling salted water and cook for 5–7 minutes; then drain on kitchen paper. Alternatively, you can place the rolls side by side on a baking sheet, brush them with egg white and bake them in a pre-heated oven at 200°C/400°F/ Gas Mark 6 for 10–12 minutes; then serve them as snacks, without sauce. Boiled rolls, which have a slightly flabby texture, need sauce; they are best served as a starter or main course.

To make the sauce, heat the stock and add the reserved meat and powder douce mixture. Simmer for several minutes to heat the meat through. Serve over the boiled rolls, re-heated if necessary.

Poached Fowl and Bacon with 'Pudding'

SERVES SIX

First stuff your capons with saveray,
With parsley, a little, hissop I say;
Then take the neck, remove the bone;
And make a pudding thereof at once
With an egg and minced bread also
With hacked liver and heart thereto . . .
Then boil the capon, as I they say,
With parsley, sage, hissop, saveray . . .
With slices of bacon embrawded here
and colour your broth with saffron dear . . .
(Mrs Groundes-Peace's Old Cookery Notebook)

1.8 kg/4 lb boiling fowl with neck and giblets

2 tablespoons finely chopped, mixed fresh savory,
parsley, hyssop and sage

Salt and pepper

700 g/1½ lb piece boiling bacon

425 ml/15 fl oz/2 cups strong dry cider

Extra herbs to garnish

'PUDDING'

Neck, liver and heart from the bird

1 teaspoonful of the herb mixture above

Salt and pepper

8 tablespoons soft white breadcrumbs

1 egg, beaten

This was a cheap and easy dish on which youngsters could practise when learning to carve poultry.

Ask a kindly poulterer to cut off the bird's head and to supply the whole neck in its skin along with the prepared bird and giblets. Mix the herbs together and put a tablespoonful aside. Add a light seasoning of salt and pepper to the rest and fill the mixture into the body cavity of the bird. Stitch or skewer the cavity openings securely. Truss the bird for boiling and place it on a trivet in a stewpan which will also hold the bacon and liquids.

To prepare the neck, ease the spine and surrounding flesh out of the skin as if peeling off a stocking. Do not break the skin. Chop the liver and heart finely and mix with half the reserved herbs, a little seasoning and the breadcrumbs. Bind with the egg. Fill this mixture into the skin, allowing room for the bread to swell. Fasten the ends of the sausage-shaped 'pudding' securely and add to the pan. (If the skin is accidentally torn, or is not supplied, you can make the stuffing into small balls and fry or bake them, as an acceptable substitute.)

Mix the cider with 425 ml/15 fl oz/2 cups water and heat until nearly boiling. Add the liquid to the pan, put on a well-fitting lid and poach the bird gently for 2–2½ hours. Add the bacon piece after 30 minutes and the stuffed neck after a further 15 minutes. Top up the pan with extra boiling water then, or later if needed.

Test the bird for readiness after 2 hours by thrusting a thin skewer into the thickest part of the thigh. The juices should run clear. A smallish bird may be almost ready by this time, and the bacon piece should be done. Take the bacon out, with the 'pudding', and leave both to rest for 10–15 minutes. Then slice both to serve as a garnish for the poached bird. Scatter a few extra herb leaves over the breast of the bird before serving.

Cream Custard Tart

SERVES SIX

*Doucetes. Take Creme a gode cupfulle, & put it on a straynour,
thanne take yolkes of Eyroun, and put ther-to, & a lytel mylke; then
strayne it throw a straynour in-to a bolle; then take Sugre y-now, &
put ther-to, or ellys hony forde faute of Sugre, than coloure it with
Safroun; than take thin cofyns, & put it in the ovynne letre, & lat hem
ben hardyd; than take a dyssche y-fastenyd on the pelys ende, & pore
thin comade in-to the dyssche, & fro the dyssche in-to the cofyns; &
whan they don a-ryse wel, teke hem out, & serue hem forth.*
(Harl. 279. p. 50.)

Pulverised dried saffron strands

Shortcrust pastry made with 225 g/8 oz flour, 65 g/2½ oz butter,
40 g/1½ oz lard, and cold water to mix

6 egg yolks

350 ml/12 fl oz/1½ cups double cream

125 ml/4 fl oz/½ cup milk

65 g/2½ oz white sugar

¼ teaspoon sea salt

I first noticed this version of the old recipe in *The Babees Book*, and it
seemed just right as a sweet dish for the youngsters being taught from
that book. There is a richer version made with almond milk for fast
days outside Lent.

Soak the saffron in 2 tablespoons water until the water is deep gold
in colour. Use the pastry to make a case 5 cm/2 inches deep in a 20-
cm/8-inch pie plate or cake tin with a loose bottom. Bake 'blind' in a
pre-heated oven at 200°C/400°F/Gas Mark 6 for 15–20 minutes,
then remove the filling of dried beans and return the case to the oven
at about 160°C/325°F/Gas Mark 3 for 6–8 minutes until dried out
and firm. Remember a cake tin is deeper than a pie plate so the case
in it may need longer baking than usual.

42. Both sheep's and goats' milk were used for butter- and cheese-making throughout medieval times.

Beat the egg yolks lightly in a bowl, then beat in the cream, milk, sugar, saffron water and salt. Pour the custard into the pastry case. Bake it at 160°C/325°F/Gas Mark 3 for about 45 minutes or until it is just set in the centre. Serve warm.

Make small tarts if you prefer. The full recipe quantity of pastry will make 36 tarts, using a 7.5 cm/3 inch cutter. You will need two thirds of the filling for them.

6

THE COURT OF RICHARD II

Richard II's Court consisted of more than just his corps of administrators and social set. The royal entourage had become, in his grandfather's long reign, a cadre of top people who shared certain new conventions and traits with their counterparts in Naples, Paris and other European courts. They were now an immensely privileged class with sophisticated tastes and great power of patronage.

This social elite used its money to buy material things. Fashion in clothes and in food and drink became important socially – and therefore politically – because the good-looking young King Richard loved both. He was fascinated by clothes, and spent a fortune on them – almost literally! Jewels, embroidery and rich fur adorned his many differently coloured jackets and gowns.

He was also reputed 'the best and ryallest vyaundier of alle cristen kynges'; in other words, the best trencherman of his generation, and the most hospitable. He was the first great magnate known to us who had a more or less comprehensive cookery book produced in English, and a distinctly luxurious book at that, to judge by the quantities of wine and saffron used in its recipes.

Being fashion-conscious meant enjoying and seeking change. Clothes grew more exaggerated in style and colour; so did foods. At the royal table, dishes were tinted a regal gold with saffron, or might be striped or chequered in varied colours. Eccentric viands titillated

43. A courtly feast: the steward calls for silence as a subtlety is brought in.

court palates, such as the strange roast, half-piglet, half-capon, called a *cokentrys*. Subtleties (the decorative dishes, presented partly as entertainment between courses at feasts) became immensely elaborate sugar-plate and marzipan sculptures in the hands of skilled royal cooks. The chronicler Hollingshead alleged that Richard had two thousand cooks. That is fanciful but his cuisine certainly became a byword for luxury.

Social behaviour also grew more extravagant. It became the 'done thing' to play at the idealised courtly living of romantic fiction, to have a safely unattainable mistress to whom one swore undying fidelity – and, in this new Court, there were plenty of suitable ladies around, with considerable influence in the disposal of favours, from small sinecures to great political offices.

The presence of ladies at Court encouraged formal courtesy and manners in every sphere of living, in dancing and singing, and other leisure activities such as hawking. Manners at meals became a matter of strict etiquette, and books of instruction were written in English, as was King Richard's cookery book, *The Forme of Cury*. Richard's

44. A great magnate, the French Duc de Berri, greets priestly guests at a formal feast, resplendent in regal robes.

courtiers were cleanly, even finicky, in their table manners – which could not be said of their politics.

King Richard had spent his boyhood watching his uncles and their followers competing for power over his person, his Court and, through it, over the country. It was probably one reason why, when he got the chance to rule himself, he made his Court larger and more grandiose than ever before. But he also did it because he enjoyed its glitter and music, its social round and romantic friendships, the gorgeous clothes he could wear and, not least, the wonderful meals he was able to eat.

Buknade (a pottage)

SERVES SIX

Buknade. Take veel, keed or hen, and boyle hem in faire water or elles in good fressh broth, and smyte hem in peces, and pike hem clene; And drawe the same broth thorgh a streynour, And cast there-to parcelly, Issope, Sauge, Maces and clowes, and lete boyle til the flessh be ynogh; and then set hit fro the fire, and aley hit vp with rawe yolkes of eyren, and cast thereto pouder ginger, and vergeous, & a litel saffron and salte, and ceson hit vppe and serue it forth. (Harl. 4016. p.85.)

2–3 sprigs each of fresh parsley and hyssop

2–3 sage leaves

1.1 litres/2 pints/5 cups chicken stock

Good pinch each of ground mace, ground cloves,
pulverised dried saffron strands and salt

350 g/12 oz cooked chicken meat without skin,
cut in small thin slices or flakes

3–4 egg yolks (depending on how rich you want your pottage)

½–1 teaspoon cider vinegar

White pepper and ground ginger to taste

Chop the herb leaves fairly finely, discarding the stems. Put the chopped leaves in a saucepan with the stock and sprinkle in the mace, cloves, saffron and salt. Bring to simmering point and add the shredded meat. Simmer until it is well heated through, while giving the egg yolks a quick beating to liquify them. Beat into them a little hot stock, then pour the mixture back into the pan and stir for a few moments over the lowest possible heat to blend and thicken the liquid slightly. Add the vinegar, pepper and ginger.

Serve as soup, or as a fairly liquid stew.

Variations
Use veal (or kid) if you wish rather than chicken, and start with raw

meat if you prefer. However, it seems foolish to go to the labour of shredding raw meat when it is easier to make a useful and pleasant dish with left-over cooked meat.

45. Chicken is the easiest meat to use for this luxurious recipe.

Roast Pheasant

SERVES SIX

Fesaunt rost. Lete a fesaunt blode in the mouth, and lete hym blede to deth; & pulle hym, and draw hym, & kutt a-wey the necke by the body, & the legges by the kne, and perbuille hym, and larde hym, and putt the knese in the vent: and rost hym, & reise hym vpp, hys legges & hys wynges as off an henne; and no sauce butt salt. (Douce 55.)

2 young pheasants

2 tablespoons unsalted butter

2 small shallots, peeled

2 rashers streaky bacon

A little seasoned flour for dredging

Sea salt

We are more humane than our ancestors where slaughtering pheasants is concerned, but the preparation of the birds for plain roasting is probably much the same. Pre-heat the oven to 200°C/400°F/Gas Mark 6. Put half the butter and a shallot inside each pheasant and cover the breast with a rasher of bacon. Wrap each bird in a separate piece of foil. Then put them side by side on a rack in a roasting-tin and roast in the oven for 30 minutes. Remove them from the oven, take off the foil and dredge with seasoned flour, baste and return to the oven for another 10 minutes, by which time they should be golden-brown. Serve with coarse sea salt in small ramekins or egg cups as a condiment or sauce.

Flavourings for Game Birds

Other 'sauces' were sometimes offered with game birds. One for pheasant consisted of white sugar with mustard powder, blended with vinegar until semi-liquid. Another, for a roasted crane, was made by combining ground black pepper, ground ginger, mustard powder, salt and vinegar. A 'sauce' of minced parsley and onions with ground garlic and vinegar was suitable for pigeons.

All these and several others may have been ways of flavouring leftovers or meat cooked for expediency – for example, needing short-term preserving – because the flesh was almost always minced before the strong 'sauce' was mixed in.

46. Pheasants were kept enclosed like domestic fowls and fattened for table.

'Roasted' Salmon with Wine Sauce

SERVES SIX

*Samon roste in Sauce. Take a Salmond, and cut him rounde, chyne
and all, and roste the pieces on a gredire; And take wyne, and pouder
of Canell, and drawe it thorgh a streynour; And take smale myced
oynons, and caste there-to, and let hem boyle; And then take vynegre
or vergeous, and pouder ginger, and cast there-to; and then ley the
samon in a dissh, and cast the sirip theron al hote, and serue it forth.
(Harl. 4016. p. 102.)*

275 ml/10 fl oz/1¼ cups medium-dry fruity white wine

175 g/6 oz small onions, peeled and finely chopped

Good pinch of ground cinnamon

¼ teaspoon white wine vinegar

Good pinch of ground ginger

6 salmon cutlets, about 2.5 cm/1 inch thick

Oil for grilling

No oil or fat is mentioned in the original recipe, but they are
suggested for frying other fish in the same manuscript. Fish must be
grilled on a greased surface whether cooked over the heat or under it
as we cook it now. Oil was the obvious medium to use, because
salmon could be eaten at Lenten meals, when strictly pious people
did not eat butter.

We do not need to 'streyne' our wine or spices today. Cook the
wine, onions and cinnamon gently in an open pan until the onions
are soft and the wine is slightly reduced. Add the vinegar and ginger,
and leave at the side of the stove. Heat the grill while you brush the
fish cutlets with oil on both sides. Grill them under moderate heat,
turning once, until just cooked. Serve each cutlet with a spoonful of
wine and onions on top.

47. Trying the new vintage wines to accompany a fine meal.

Decorated Meatballs

MAKES 18 MEATBALLS

Pumpes. Take an sethe a gode gobet of Porke, & not to lene, as tendyr as thou may; than take hem vppe & choppe hem as smal as thou may; than take clowes & Maces, & choppe forth with—alle, & Also choppe forth with Roysonys of coraunce; than take hem & rolle hem as round as thou may, lyke to smale pelettys, a ij inches a-bowte, than ley hem on a dysshe be hem selue; than make a gode Almounde mylke, & a lye it with floure of Rys, & lat it boyle wyl, but loke that it be clene rennyng, & at the dressoure, ley v pompys in a disshe, & pore thin potage ther-on. An if thou wolt, sette on euery pompe a flos campy flour, & a-boue straw on Sugre y-now, & Maces; & serue hem forth. And sum men make the pellettys of vele or beeff, but Porke ys beste & fayrest. (Harl. 279. p.31.)

900 g/2 lb lean pork without skin or bone

1.1 litres/2 pints/5 cups beef stock, skimmed of fat

125 g/4 oz ground almonds

1 tablespoon rice flour or cornflour

1 tablespoon currants

¼ teaspoon ground mace

⅛ teaspoon ground cloves

Salt and pepper

A little oil for greasing

GARNISH

White sugar and ground mace for sprinkling

Small real or dried flowers

Wild marjoram (oregano) or other culinary herbs when in bloom add scent as well as colour to any dish they decorate.

These meatballs can be used as snacks for two or three people, or as a garnish for roast poultry or game. Cook the pork in the stock until just about tender. Drain it, reserving the stock. Use 275 ml/10 fl oz/1¼ cups of the stock to make almond 'milk' with the ground almonds and rice flour or cornflour as described on page 64. Put this and the rest of the stock aside, separately, to cool.

Cut the pork into small slices. It should still be moist but not pink. Process the slices in batches in an electric blender, adding the currants, spices and seasoning while processing. Form the mixture into 18 meatballs about 4 cm/1½ inches in diameter. Roll these in a lightly greased frying-pan until lightly browned all over, then leave to cool. Thin down the almond 'milk' if necessary with a little stock; it should coat the meatballs lightly. Cover each meatball with a little 'sauce'. Just before serving, sprinkle the dish lightly with white sugar and the golden mace, and decorate it with small vivid flowers.

Golden Steamed Custard

SERVES SIX

Letelorye. Take ayren and wryng hem thurgh a straynour, and do therto cowe mylke, with butter and safroun and salt. Seeth it wel; leshe it, and loke that it be stondyng, and serue it forth. (Cl. IV. 83.)

575 ml/1 pint/2½ cups milk

Good pinch of dried saffron strands

4 eggs

¼ teaspoon sea salt

1–2 teaspoons butter

Medieval aristocrats may have enjoyed custard with pools of melted butter on top, but modern diners usually do not. I have therefore kept the butter suggested in the old recipe to a minimum.

Warm the milk to hand-hot and sprinkle in the saffron. Beat the eggs until liquid and frothy, adding the salt while beating. Then stir in the milk. Use the butter to grease a 1-litre/1¾-pint/4½-cup soufflé dish or similar square dish and pour in the custard. Cover the dish tightly with doubled greased foil. Place it in a saucepan and pour into the pan enough scalding-hot water to come half-way up the sides of the dish. Place the pan over low heat so that the water barely bubbles; cover the pan and steam the custard for 1–1½ hours or until fairly firm in the middle. Let it cool completely, when it should be firm enough to cut in wedges or slices. It can be served with a savoury topping, such as crumbled fried cod's roe or sliced leeks, either as a starter or a light supper dish. Alternatively it makes a pleasant mild dessert when topped with a fresh fruit purée.

If you prefer, you can bake the custard. Stand the dish in a roasting-pan and add enough hot water to 'jacket' the bottom half of the dish. Bake at 150°C/300°F/Gas Mark 2 for 45 minutes, then raise the heat to 160°C/325°F/Gas Mark 3 until the custard is set.

48. A sturdy housewife buying eggs.

Rose Pudding

SERVES SIX

Rosee. Take thyk milke; sethe it. Cast therto sugur, a gode porcioun; pynes, dates ymynced, canel, & powdour gynger; and seeth it, and alye it with flours of white rosis, and flour of rys. Cole it; salt it & messe it forth. If thou wilt in stede of almounde mylke, take swete crem of kyne. (CI. IV. 53.)

Petals of one full-blown but unshrivelled white rose

4 level tablespoons rice flour or cornflour

275 ml/10 fl oz/1¼ cups milk

50 g/2 oz caster sugar

¾ teaspoon ground cinnamon

¾ teaspoon ground ginger

575 ml/20 fl oz/2½ cups single cream

Pinch of salt

10 dessert dates, stoned and finely chopped

1 tablespoon chopped pine nut kernels

'Thyk milke' in the old recipe looks suspiciously like sour milk or curd cheese, but in fact it means rich almond 'milk' for a 'fasting' meal. Hastily cream is offered as an alternative for other diners.

Take the petals off the rose one by one, and snip off the end which was attached to the seed-case. Blanch the petals in boiling water for 2 minutes, then press them between several sheets of soft kitchen paper and put a heavy flat weight on top to squeeze them dry. (They may look depressingly greyish but blending will cure the dish's complexion.) Put the rice flour or cornflour in a saucepan, and blend into it enough of the milk to make a smooth cream. Stir in the remaining milk. Place the pan over low heat, and stir until the mixture starts to thicken. Turn it into the goblet of an electric blender, and add the sugar, spices and rose-petals. Process until fully blended, then add and blend in the cream and salt.

Turn the mixture into a heavy saucepan, and stir over very low heat, below the boil, until it is the consistency of softly whipped cream. Stir in most of the chopped dates and pine nut kernels, and stir for 2 minutes more. Turn into a glass or decorative bowl and cool. Stir occasionally while cooling to prevent a skin forming. Chill. Just before serving decorate with the remaining dates and nuts.

49. A white rose pleases all the senses (even that of taste).

7

COURTLY AND CHRISTMAS FEASTING

The inner circle of the Court 'in attendance' on the King included most departments of the royal household; with their associates, staff, followers and hangers-on they formed a group at least some hundreds strong. Since everyone had to depend basically on local foodstuffs, this crowd had to move periodically in a cumbersome cavalcade from one royal palace to another before supplies ran out. Those who made the arrangements lived in a constant state of preparing for the next flit. For the two great Feasts at Easter and Christmas, preparations had to start months ahead when preserves were ordered and made, hay and straw for men's pallets and horse-feed were harvested, and cattle were slaughtered. November's Martlemas beef made Easter Sunday's dinner. (Martinmas, the feast of St Martin, is on 11 November.)

When royalty shifted to where the Christmas Feast would take place, great wagons went ahead carrying heavier equipment and bulk materials; and the cooks' gear was transported too in heavy carts – just when the cooks needed their spices most, because the Advent fast had probably just begun. That meant four weeks of lean eating to prepare one for the Feast.

Since the 'top brass' assembling for Christmas were among the most pampered consumers in the known world, their so-called fasting was not usually very serious. But that did not prevent them looking forward to Christmas as a release from stringent self-discipline.

The Christmas holiday lasted only a few half-days for most people, because the usual daily farm and other labourers' work and household chores went on, and not all employers gave much time off. But courtly folk had ample leisure to display their new headgear at one party after another over nearly a fortnight of intermittent feasting, and to enjoy the colourful, scented delights of top-class cuisine; even if their lowly rank entitled them on full-scale royal occasions to only two of the three courses, and to a limited choice of dishes (squires, pages, local burgesses and so on were allowed only one course). There were sometimes entertainments to watch while waiting, and the *entremets* or subtleties to admire, especially if their labels were read aloud. The boar's head brought in by carol singers at the Twelfth Night feast was a popular *entremet*, and so was the peacock, proudly displayed regnant and bedecked on its platters.

Most of the entertainments were showy as well. The tumblers and minstrels were paid entertainers of high quality. So too were the mummers in curious costumes who acted in verse. Court youths appeared as 'disguisers', even more outrageously dressed, who did not speak but offered themselves as dance partners. When Richard II was king, he might take part himself, although luckily his costly elaborate clothes always identified him. Those who partnered him hoped to be able to perform well for him with the sweetmeats on the table to sustain them, and the spiced wine and cheese going round.

Entertainment was the main part of any feast, especially a great one; and at the end, when the alms baskets were carried out to the poor and the last Twelfth Night toast was drunk, it was to be hoped that one and all could say, 'That was a good feast. The year ahead will go well!'

50. A royal occasion – John of Gaunt dines with two kings and four bishops.

Broiled Venison

SERVES SIX

The syde of a dere of hie grece. Wesch hem, do hem on a broch. Scotch hem ovyrtwarte & ayenne crosswyse in the maner of losyngys in the flesch syde. Rost hym; take redde wyn, poudyr of gynger, poudyr of pepyr & salt, and bast hit till hit be thorow. Have a chargeour undyrneth & kepe the fallyng, and bast hit therwith ayene. Then take hit of & smyte hit as thu lyst & serve hit forth. (OP. 159.)

6 × 1-cm/½-inch-thick slices venison fillet or haunch

Bacon fat or lard for rubbing

Pepper sauce for veal or venison to serve

BASTING SAUCE

350 ml/12 fl oz/1½ cups red wine

3 tablespoons oil

⅛ teaspoon ground ginger

Salt and black pepper

Venison fillet was the most prized cut. It might be scored in lozenge shapes with a knife point or parboiled and larded with salt pork before being spit-roasted whole. Modern farmed venison, however, seems to be tenderised better by being marinated.

Combine all the basting sauce ingredients and soak the venison slices in the sauce for at least 2–3 hours; elderly meat will need longer. Pour off the sauce into a jug when you are ready to cook. Put the meat on a board and pat it dry, then nick the edges of the slices and rub them all over with the fat.

Thread the slices on skewers or lay them on a greased grill grid. Heat the grill to medium-high and grill the meat like steak until medium-rare or well done as you wish. (For well-done meat, reduce the temperature after searing both sides and cook slowly.) Baste the meat with the reserved basting sauce while cooking and turn it once using a fish slice; do not prod it with a fork. When done, transfer the slices to a warmed serving platter, and serve at once, with the hot Pepper Sauce in a sauce boat.

51. Venison for a great Christmas feast.

Pepper Sauce for Veal or Venison
SERVES SIX

Piper for feel and for venysoun. Take brede, and frye it in grece, draw it vp with brothe and vinegre: caste ther-to poudre piper, and salt, sette on the fire, boile it, and melle it forthe. (Ashmole, p. 110.)

5 slices soft-grain white bread, crusts removed

Dripping from roast veal or venison, or butter

575 ml/1 pint/2½ cups juices from roast meat or stock

2 tablespoons red wine vinegar

½ teaspoon ground black pepper

Sprinkling of salt

Fry the bread slices in the dripping or other fat until light gold. Break them into small pieces and put them in the goblet of an electric blender with all the other ingredients. Process until fully blended. Turn the mixture into a small pan and simmer for 2–3 minutes, stirring. Taste and add any extra pepper needed to make it pungent but not fierce. Serve it in a warmed sauce boat with veal or venison.

Pork Roast with Spiced Wine

SERVES SIX

Cormarye. Take colyaundre, caraway smale grounden, powdour of peper and garlec ygrounde, in rede wyne; medle alle thise togyder and salt it. Take loynes of pork rawe and fle of the skyn, and pryk it wel with a knyf, and lay it in the sawse. Roost it whan thou wilt, & kepe that that fallith therfro in the rostyng and seeth it in a possynet with faire broth, & serue it forth with the roost anoon. (CI. IV. 54.)

1.8 kg/4 lb pork loin joint on the bone

1½ teaspoons ground coriander

1 teaspoon caraway seeds, pounded or pulverised in a grinder

1 large clove garlic, peeled and crushed with salt

½ teaspoon freshly ground black pepper

1 teaspoon salt

175 ml/6 fl oz/¾ cup red wine

About 225 ml/8 fl oz/1 cup chicken stock

The spiced wine was originally used as a marinade or baste dripped over the meat while it spit-roasted. A joint might also be heavily dredged with crumbs or flour while it roasted, or might be wrapped in caul like a huge sausage to prevent the surface scorching. I have used foil for wrapping, which makes it easy to save the drippings. Ask your butcher to chine the joint.

A small coffee or nut mill will reduce the caraway seeds to powder, and do it more effectively if you grind the garlic with them.

Pre-heat the oven to 220°C/425°F/Gas Mark 7. Strip the skin off the pork joint and prick the fat all over with a knife point. Mix the spices, garlic and seasonings into the wine and rub the meat all over with this mixture. Lay the joint on a doubled sheet of foil big enough to enclose it. Fasten the edges of the foil around the meat, leaving an open space at the top. Pour most of the remaining wine mixture over

52. Dispatching the Christmas boar.

the meat, then close the foil parcel. Cook the joint at 220°C/425°F/ Gas Mark 7 for 10 minutes, then reduce the heat to 180°C/350°F/Gas Mark 4; allow 30 minutes per 450 g/1 lb and 30 minutes over. Open the foil for the last 30 minutes to brown the surface of the meat; turn up the heat a little if you wish.

Lift the meat carefully out of the foil parcel and 'rest' it on a warmed serving dish while you make a sauce with the spiced wine. Scrape any drippings and wine mixture from the foil into a saucepan and stir in the chicken stock. Simmer it for a few moments, then taste. Adjust the seasoning if required, strain into a warmed gravy boat and serve with the meat.

A Grete Pye

SERVES SIX TO EIGHT

Grete pyes. Take faire yonge beef, And suet of a fatte beste, or of
Motton, and hak all this on a borde small; and caste therto pouder of
peper and salt; and whan it is small hewen, put hit in a bolle, And
medle hem well; then make a faire large Cofyn, and couche som of this
stuffur in. Then take Capons, Hennes, Mallardes, Connynges, and
parboile hem clene; take wodekokkes, teles, grete briddes, and plom
hem in a boiling pot; And then couche al this fowle in the Coffyn, And
put in euerych of hem a quantite of pouder of peper and salt. Then take
mary, harde yolkes of egges, Dates cutte in ij peces, reisons of
coraunce, prunes, hole clowes, hole maces, Canell and saffron. But
first, whan thoug hast cowched all thi foule, ley the remenaunt of thyne
other stuffur of beef a-bought hem, as thou thenkest goode; and then
strawe on hem this: dates, mary, and reysons, &c. And then close thi
Coffyn with a lydde of the same paast, And putte hit in the oven, And
late hit bake ynough; but be ware, or thou close hit, that there come no
saffron nygh the brinkes there-of, for then hit wol neuer close.
(Harl. 4016. p.76.)

450 g/1 lb shortcrust pastry

1 egg white, beaten until liquid

450 g/1 lb boned breasts of chicken, pigeon or wild duck
and/or saddle of hare or rabbit (not stewing meat)

Salt and black pepper

450 g/1 lb minced beef

2 tablespoons shredded suet

3 hard-boiled egg yolks, crumbled

Spice mixture made with ¼ teaspoon each ground cinnamon
and mace and a pinch of ground cloves

25 g/1 oz stoned cooking dates, chopped

25 g/1 oz currants

50 g/2 oz stoned prunes, soaked and drained

125 ml/4 fl oz/½ cup beef stock

1 tablespoon rice flour or cornflour

No Christmas feast in medieval times was complete without a 'grete pye'. In some recipes, it could contain many varied meats, but quite often only two or three different kinds were suggested; change the meats suggested here if you wish.

Use just over half the pastry to line a 23-cm/9-inch pie plate. Brush the inside with some of the egg white.

Skin the pieces of breast and other meat if necessary and parboil them gently in salted water for 10–15 minutes. Drain and leave to cool. Mix together in a bowl the minced beef, suet, salt and pepper to taste, the egg yolks and half the spice mixture. Add the rest of the spices to the dried fruit in another bowl. Slice the parboiled meat. Pre-heat the oven to 220°C/425°F/Gas Mark 7.

Add 1 or 2 tablespoons of the beef stock to the rice flour or cornflour in a small saucepan and cream them together; then add the remaining stock and stir over gentle heat until slightly thickened. Keep aside.

Cover the bottom of the pastry case with half the mince mixture. Arrange the sliced meat in a flat layer on top. Scatter the chopped spiced fruit over it and cover with the remaining mince. Pour the thickened stock over the lot.

Roll out the remaining pastry into a round to make a lid for the pie. Brush the rim of the case with a little more egg white and cover with the lid. Press the edges to seal, and make escape slits for steam. Decorate with the pastry trimmings and glaze with egg white. Bake for 15 minutes, then reduce the heat to 160°C/325°F/Gas Mark 3 and bake for 45–50 minutes longer.

53. The most splendid of wine cups – the Royal Gold Cup of the kings of England and France.

Piment

SERVES TWELVE TO SIXTEEN

Pur fait ypocras. Troys vnces de canell & iii vnces gyngeuer; spykenard de Spayn, le pays dun denerer; garyngale, clowes gylofre, poeure long, noiey mugadey, mayioyame, cardemonii, de chescun i quarter donce; grayne de paradys, flour de queynel, de chescun dm. vnce; de tout soit fait powdour &c. (Cl. IV. 199.)

2 litres/3½ pints/8¾ cups red wine

175 g/6 oz white sugar

1 tablespoon ground cinnamon

¾ tablespoon ground ginger

1 teaspoon each ground cloves, grated nutmeg, marjoram (fresh if possible), ground cardamom, ground black pepper and a pinch of grated galingale (if available)

I have called this a piment – a general name for sweetened spiced wines – rather than hypocras because the long pepper (*poeure long*) and the grains of paradise (*grayne de paradis*) in the old recipe are virtually unobtainable today. So is Spikenard (*spykenard*).

Warm the wine until just beginning to steam. Add the sugar and allow to dissolve. Mix all the spices and herbs together. Stir half this mixture into the wine, then taste and slowly add more until you achieve a flavour you like (you will probably need most or all of the mixture). Simmer your 'mix' very gently for 10 minutes. Strain through a jelly bag (which may take some hours). Bottle when cold, then cork securely. Use within 1 week.

CLARY

Pine Nut Candy

Payn ragoun. Take hony and sugur cipre and clarifie it togydre, and boile it with esy fyre, and kepe it wel fro brennyng. And whan it hath yboiled a while, take vp a drope therof with thy fyngur and do it in a litel water, and loke if it hong togydre; and take it fro the fyre and do therto pynes the thriddendele & powdour gyngeuer, and stere it togyder til it bigynne to thik, and cast it on a wete table; lesh it and serue it forth with fryed mete, on flessh dayes or on fisshe dayes. (CI. IV. 68.)

200 g/7 oz fine white sugar

2 tablespoons clear honey

125 ml/4 fl oz/½ cup water

1 heaped tablespoon pine nut kernels, chopped small or ground

100 g/3½ oz fine soft white breadcrumbs

½–1 teaspoon ground ginger

This recipe contains a 'mystery' ingredient, the *thriddendele*, or third item, which seems to have been used to give the sweetmeat a bread-

54. All sorts of dishes from soup to sweetmeats graced Sir Geoffrey Luttrell's table.

like texture. I have used soft white breadcrumbs with the pine nut kernels mentioned in the old recipe; you can use more ground nuts and fewer crumbs if cost allows.

In the original recipe this very sweet candy is served with *'fryed mete'* on a flesh *or* a fish day: so perhaps that *'mete'* was *'mylk rost'* – that is, a sweet omelet or custard fritters.

Put the sugar, honey and water in a deep pan and cook over low heat until a sugar thermometer placed in it registers 110°C/230°F. At once turn the syrup into a chilled bowl and beat it hard for 2–3 minutes; then beat in the remaining ingredients. Turn the mixture into a wetted shallow tin and leave to harden. Cut into small pieces to serve.

Lombard Slices

SERVES SIX

Auter maner leche lumbarde. Take fayre Hony, and clarifi yt on the
fyre tylle it wexe hard; then take hard yolkys of Eyroun, & kryme a
gode quantyte ther-to tyl it be styf y-now; an thenne take it vppe, & ley
it on a borde; then take fayre gratyd Brede, and pouder pepir, & molde
it to-gederys with thine hondys, tyl it be so styf that it wole ben lechyd;
than leche it; then take wyne & pouder Gyngere, Canelle, & a lytil
claryfyid hony, & late renne thorw a straynour, & caste this Syrip ther-
on, when thou shalt serue it out instede of Clerye.
(Harl. 279. p. 35 vj.)

12 hard-boiled egg yolks (see method)

8 tablespoons clear honey

175 g/6 oz fine white breadcrumbs or as needed

Pinch of ground black pepper

SYRUP

225 ml/8 fl oz/1 cup red wine

Good pinch of ground cinnamon and ginger

5 tablespoons clear honey

55. A honey bee.

There are at least three recipes for the sweetmeat called Leche Lumbard, one stiffened with dates, one with almonds and this one with egg yolks. If you want to, you can use fewer egg yolks and more breadcrumbs, but the consistency will not be as smooth.

Sieve the egg yolks on to a sheet of paper. Bring the honey for the slices to the boil and simmer for 2 minutes. Take the pan off the heat. Add the sieved yolks little by little to the pan, beating or stirring rapidly to blend them in smoothly. Then blend in the breadcrumbs and pepper; use sufficient breadcrumbs to make the mixture stiff enough to mould. Shape it into a brick and chill until cold and firm. Cut it into small slices like halva.

Simmer the ingredients for the syrup until the wine is well reduced. Spoon a little over each slice before serving.

Serve with small spoons as a sweet mouthful with coffee.

8

OF HERBALS AND SIMPLES

One of the housewife's main cares in the Middle Ages was her household's health. She had to grow, combine and use the herbs needed for dosing her family and servants, and clean and bandage such wounds as she could. Her simples (medicinal herbs) produced commonsense cures for many everyday troubles, based on long experience and often helped by a dose of folk magic. But when her own efforts failed she could usually find professional help, if she could pay for it.

There was, first, the local Wise Woman, some of whose nostrums relied, like the housewife's own, on her patient's credulity, but who knew many time-tested herbal cures besides. Then there were three more scholarly sources of aid. The most helpful might often be a community of local monks or nuns who, among their labours, maintained an infirmary and hospice for invalids or lepers, the casualties of brutality or the aged infirm. Caring for the sick was a Christian duty, part and parcel of the alms-giving which fed the beggar at the gate as far as the monastery could afford to do it. (By the fifteenth century, many could not.)

The almoner of a secular nobleman, unlike his religious counter-part, probably also regarded a healthy work force as an investment, and for that reason kept a first-aid kit and a few drugs handy, if no more.

Another secular source of drugs was the apothecary's shop. Unlike a modern pharmacist, an apothecary could sell to whom he chose, and many had (or pretended to have) as much knowledge as a licensed doctor concerning the use of their wares. Besides medicinal drugs, they sold alcoholic spirits and several delicious forms of sugar (then considered a spice) for medicinal use. There were little twisted sugar-sticks called *penidia*, and rose or violet-scented sugar, appropriately coloured, regarded as cures for coughs and consumption. But these medicinal sugars, like the distillates used by students of alchemy and cooks, were very expensive indeed.

The alchemist and the astrologer had both influenced the doctor's training. Whether he had been schooled in London, Paris or Salerno, he had to know the lore of the stars and how they affected humans and herbs. This knowledge tied in with the doctrines of Galen, the Greek physician who had practised in Rome towards the end of the first century AD; his teaching still dictated how the doctor viewed people and diagnosed their ills. The classical Greek theories, in their turn, were derived from the papyri of ancient Egypt.

Luckily not all physicians, or ordinary citizens for that matter, accepted the ancient teachings holus-bolus. The Goodman of Paris might be superstitious about when to plant parsley, but he knew well enough how to spot a malingerer among his workers. Chaucer, in the *Prologue* to *The Canterbury Tales*, turned a cynical eye on the doctor who claimed to diagnose by astrology while conspiring with his apothecaries to defraud his patients. Monks who made medicines knew that their spirituous indigestion mixtures might be put to other uses; and although herbals and leechbooks made large claims, many doctors must have known that a fair number of their more curious cures were just placebos.

The medicinal recipes I have chosen as samples here come from a fifteenth-century collection, called *A Leechbook*, which has belonged to the Medical Society of London since 1773 or soon after. This collection consists of no fewer than 1074 recipes covering an amazingly wide range of ailments; and the scholarly modern editor and transcriber has had the stamina to add an Appendix of forty-six more, including some veterinary receipts, from the early Tudor period. Between them they provide a daunting choice, although

56. This frontispiece of a well-known herbal shows two saints reputed to be doctors who had been martyred for treating people without charging – and for curing – them.

luckily, it has proved reasonably easy to resolve in this particular book. Since it is a cookbook and will, I hope, be used a lot, it was obviously wise to focus on ills resulting from over-indulgence, and on cures using the plants and spices which grew or could be gained in our own countryside and gardens in the fifteenth century. This I have done, making my choice more on a pin-pricking basis than with any skill, but fascinated to find how many of the herbs are used by trained, practising medical herbalists today, and quite often for the same reasons as their medieval forebears.

I have been assured that the medical recipes I have chosen are innocuous; but, unlike the cookery recipes, these are *not* intended for trying out on yourself or anyone else, certainly not without medical supervision. I have not tested them myself.

I have not tried either the recipe for cleaning and whitening the teeth, or the still-room receipts for making rose and nut oils which I have added after the medical recipes mainly because I find them delightful, innocent conceits.

Because the recipes as Mr Warren Dawson has transcribed them are already quite clear, I have not rewritten them in modern form. Rather, I have added a few notes about the herbal and other ingredients to each transcribed recipe.

57. A cheerful patient and his complacent doctors.

For the Migraine

Take half a dishful of barley, one handful each of betony, vervain, and other herbs that are good for the head; and when they be well boiled together, take them up and wrap them in a cloth and lay them to the sick head, and it shall be whole. I proved. (MS 136. 60 g. Trs. W.D.)

I suppose that a rotten sick headache might be eased by a poultice of hot barley and herbs. Betony was a favourite herb in the Middle Ages and was taken internally for many ailments. Today it is still used mainly for nervous headaches and some types of migraine. It contains the alkaloids betonicine, stachydrine and trigonelline.

Vervain is also used nowadays as a nervine (a nerve tonic), and is a good calming restorative for a patient who is in a debilitated condition. It is used in cases of migraine and depression. Its main constituents are a variety of glycosides (including some reputedly cardio-active ones) and a bitter irridoid.

58. A professional apothecary making medicines.

For the Colic

Take may-butter of the amount of a nut, five blades [stamens] of saffron, and cut the saffron small, and mingle it with the butter. And put it in the navel of the sick. And take the earth that is upon a threshold to the amount of the palm of a man's hand, and lay it on coals of fire, and sprinkle thereon dregs of good ale. And turn it and sprinkle it thereupon [on the fire] till it be hot through, and then take it up and lay it in a linen cloth and bind it to the navel. And lay it over the butter and saffron, and so put it on the navel. And he shall be whole. (MS 136. 1061. Trs. W.D)

Another poultice recipe! This one is a good deal nastier than it sounds. May butter was made for children by setting newly made, unsalted butter on open platters in the sun for almost a fortnight. By that time it was stinking rancid, colourless and devoid of vitamin A, although it did contain increased vitamin D as a result of the action of the sun's rays. (It may therefore have helped children with rickets or pains in the joints.)

The saffron sounds costly but five stamens would probably not have broken the bank for a reasonably affluent client who could afford linen wrappings. It was used as a carminative (cure for flatulence) besides its use as a regal colouring agent in food.

To avoid Wind that is the Cause of Colic

Take cumin and anise, of each equally much, and lay it in white wine to steep, and cover it over with wine, and let it stand still so three days and three nights. And then let it be taken out and laid upon an ash-board for to dry nine days and to be turned about. And at the nine days' end, take and put it in an earthen pot and dried over the fire, and then make powder thereof. And then eat it in pottage or drink it, and it shall void the wind that is cause of colic. (MS. 136. 1071. Trs. W.D.)

It should indeed 'void wind' because anise, like cumin, is a carminative. Among their other uses, these two herbs, together with fennel and dill, were often used in the past with strong purgatives to relieve the resultant griping pains. Wind and constipation were a common preoccupation in the Middle Ages, one suspects because people ate so many pulses and so few fresh vegetables except cabbage.

For a Man that is Sick in his Stomach

Take cumin a pound, and bray it in a mortar; and take the same and good stale ale, and seethe them together, and skim it well. And when it is well boiled, take it from the fire, and let it run through a strainer or through a linen cloth, and let the sick drink the licour lukewarm. And the dross of the cumin so boiled to be put in a bag of linen cloth shaped like a heart, and to be laid to the stomach of him that is sick, as hot as he may suffer it. (MS 136. 1069. Trs. W.D.)

59. A lay sister making a vinous potion.

60. Strong spirits!

Cumin is not commonly grown in our herb gardens now, but in the fifteenth century it was more popular than the other familiar herbal cures for flatulence, fennel and dill. It was also traditionally well known as a digestive tonic and a remedy for colic. Cumin poultices were used for stomach cramps and stitch as recently as sixty years ago.

Ale was always left to clear itself, and poor folk often got cheap ale thick with dregs which had not yet settled. Brewers were not supposed to sell ale less than forty-eight hours old, so the term 'good stale ale' meant top-quality stuff – preferably only thick with the herbs strained out of it before it was drunk. Putting the residues into a heart-shaped bag was a practical as well as a pleasingly ingenious idea, given the shape of the human belly.

Whatever the cause of a stomach upset, cleaning the teeth freshened the whole mouth, and revived a person's confidence with it. This is the simplest tooth-cleaning recipe in the *Leechbook*.

To cleanse [teeth] and make them white. Take the root of mallows and rub thy teeth and thy gums therewith. And after that take a rough cloth, and rub thy teeth therewith. If thou washest thy mouth once a month with water or with wine that titemall, that is spurge, is seethed in, the teeth shall never fall. Knotgrass kneaded and laid to the teeth is a good medicine. (MS. 136. 907. Trs. W.D.)

Accidents as well as lapses in discipline could require treatment. A blow or a fall perhaps!

To Stanch Blood at the Nose

At least five recipes are given in the *Leechbook*. Here are two of them:

Anoint the nose with the juice of leeks within . . . Also dandelion will stanch blood at the nose, if thou wilt break it, and hold it to the nose that the savour may go into it. (MS. 136. 833. Trs. W.D.)

Blood-letting, in moderation, was considered almost a panacea in the Middle Ages, so it is interesting to see herbal remedies being used to stem the flow of blood in this case. Herbs were also used to curb an excess menstrual flow and other forms of unwanted loss of blood.

The *Leechbook* contains a good many simple herbal remedies for undramatic ailments like nose-bleeds. But perhaps the most useful is not for an ailment at all; in an age when central heating was unknown and fires were banked at night, this recipe may well have been a godsend:

How a Man should keep him from cold. Seethe nettle-seed and oil and anoint the feet and hands, and it will keep away the cold. (MS. 136. 236. Trs. W.D.)

135

61. Blood-letting was often thought a panacea for all ills.

One could prepare for winter days too by conserving herb and nut oils in summer and autumn, capturing roses, for instance, when most sweetly scented and green herbs at their most healthful. Oils for cooking, oils for rubbing!

Oil of almonds. Put them in hot water and blanch them, and stamp them, and put them in a pot; and set that pot on another seething pot, and the breath (steam) of the seething pot shall rise and enter into the kernels or into the almonds. And that will become oil when it is wrung through a cloth. Also thou may do in the same wise, of the kernels of filbert-nuts and walnuts. (MS. 136. 669. Trs. W.D.)

62. The spirit of Nature shows a lover a rose. Roses were used to make a curative rubbing oil, which must have made the whole hall fragrant.

Oil of roses is made of oil of olive and of roses hanging together in a glass vessel thirty days or forty, in the sun. But it is better to seethe the roses and the oil together over the fire, and cleanse it and keep it.
(MS. 136. 678. Trs. W.D)

For to make oil of sage and of parsley. Seethe them in oil of olive till it be thick and green. And this is good for sharp pains in joints, and aching. (MS. 136. 670. Trs. W.D.)

Then, lastly, a recipe for achieving 'continual good health' by commonsense advice which (if followed) would save the average party-goer from crass folly if no more.

All bitter things comfort the stomach. All sweet things enfeeble it. Roasted things are dry. All raw things annoy the stomach. Whoso will keep continual health, [must] keep his stomach so that he put not too much therein when he hath appetite, nor take anything into it when he hath no need. And then continual health will ensue.
(MS. 136. 1019. Trs. W.D.)

PARSLEY

BIBLIOGRAPHY
AND MANUSCRIPT ABBREVIATIONS

The following list includes the printed transcripts of manuscripts used in the compilation of this book, and certain other books which have been invaluable research material. The old recipes quoted in the text are labelled by abbreviations of the titles of the manuscripts from which they derive; these abbreviations are given below after the full titles.

Old Recipe Collections

The Goodman of Paris. Translated into English by Eileen Power. George Routledge and Sons 1928. *MP. Trans. E. Power.*

A Leechbook or Collection of Medical Recipes of the Fifteenth Century. The text of MS 136 of the Literary Society of London. Transcribed and edited by Warren R. Dawson FRCE, FRSL, FSA Scotland. Macmillan and Co. Ltd 1934. *MS 136. Trs. W.D.* 236, 609, 669, 670, 678, 833, 907, 1019, 1061, 1069, 1071.

Two Fifteenth-Century Cookery Books. Harleian MS 279 and Harleian MS 4016 with extracts from Ashmole MS 1439, Laud MS 553 and Douce MS 55. Edited by Thomas Austin. Oxford University Press 1964 (reprint). *Ashmole 1439*. p. 110; *Douce 55*. p. 116; *Harl. 279*. pp. 31, 35, 40, 46, 50, 76, 85, 102; *Harl. 4016*. pp. 72, 79, 101; *Laud. 553*. p. 114.

Mrs Groundes-Peace's Old Cookery Notebooks; transcript in verse of material from *Liber Cure Cocorum*. Compiled by Zara Groundes-Peace, edited by Robin Howe. David and Charles for the International Wine and Food Publishing Company/Rainbird Reference Books 1971. *Mrs Groundes-Peace's Old Cookery Notebook.*

Curye on Inglysch. Five MS collections of fourteenth-/fifteenth-century recipes, edited by Constance B. Hieatt and Sharon Butler. Oxford University Press 1985. *CI.I.* 56; *CI.III.* 26, 28, 33; *CI.IV.* 1, 2, 6, 18, 23, 24, 50, 53, 54, 68, 71, 82, 83, 85, 89, 103, 157, 188, 199.

An Ordinance of Pottage. Fifteenth-century recipes in Yale University's MS Beinecke 163. Edited by Constance B. Hieatt, with a commentary and adapted modern recipes. Prospect Books 1988. *OP.* 29, 159.

Antiquitates Culinariae 1791. Revd Richard Warner. Facsimile edition of Prospect Books. The book includes *Warner's Preliminary Discourse, The Forme of Cury, Ancient Cookery*, etc. *FC. Antiq. Cul.* 50.

Books Used as Sources

The Babees Book: John Russell's Book of Nurture. Annotated and edited by F. J. Furnivall MA. Greenwood Press 1969 (reprint).

The Canterbury Tales (2 vols). Translated into modern English by Nevill Coghill. Folio Society 1956.

Other Reference Material

Buxton, Moira *Medieval Cooking Today*. Kylin Press 1983.

Sir Gawain and the Green Knight. Translated by Keith Harrison. Folio Society 1983.

Henisch, Bridget Ann *Fast and Feast: Food in Medieval Society*. Pennsylvania State University Press 1976.

Hieatt, Constance B. and Butler, Sharon *Pleyn Delit: Medieval Cookery for Modern Cooks*. University of Toronto Press 1976.

Lafarge, M. W. *A Baronial Household of the Thirteenth Century*. Harvester Press 1980.

Mathew, G. *The Court of Richard II*. 1968.

Mead, W. E. *The English Medieval Feast*. George Allen & Unwin 1967.

Myers, A. R. *England in the Late Middle Ages*. Penguin Books 1985 (reprint).

The Paston Letters. Edited by Norman Davis. Clarendon Press 1958.

Power, Eileen *Medieval Women*. Edited by M. M. Postan. Cambridge University Press 1984 (reprint).

Stenton, D. M. *English Society in the Early Middle Ages*. Penguin Books 1985 (reprint).

Wilson, C. Anne *Food and Drink in Britain*. Constable & Co. 1973.

PHOTOGRAPHIC ACKNOWLEDGEMENTS

The numbers refer to the figure numbers.
Archivi Alinari SpA, Florence: 1; Bibliothèque Nationale, Paris: 3 (MS 01 fr. 616, f.67), 40; The Bodleian Library, Oxford: 8 (Bodley 264, f.170v), 13 (Canon Lit. 99, f.16r); British Library, London: frontispiece (MS 24098, f.19v), 4 (Harleian 4425, f.14), 7 (from a drawing by Edward Blore, Add 42019, f.95), 9 (Add 42130, f.176v), 12 (Royal 18 D II, f.148), 16 (IB 55242 bbIII), 20 (Royal 10 E IV, f.222v), 21 and back cover (Sloane 2435, f.44v), 24 (Add 42130, f.16), 28 (Add 38126, f.145v), 30 (MS 19720, f.165), 32 (*Tacunium Sanitatis*), 34 (Harley 2838, f.37), 36 (Royal E III, f.36), 37 (Burney 275, f.94), 38 (Add 34294, f.138b), 39 (C31C7, frontis.), 41 (Add 34294, f.138b), 42 (Kings 24, f.37), 45 (from *Tacunium Sanitatis*), 46 (Harley 7026, f.5v), 47 (Add 24098, f.27v), 48 (IB 55242 bbIII), 50 (Royal 14 E IV, f.284), 52 (Add 18850, f.12), 54 (Add 42130, f.208), 57 (Royal 15 E II, f.77v), 59 (Royal 15 D I, f.1), 60 (IB 55242 bbIII), 61 (Sloane 2435, f.11v), 62 (Harley 4425, f.36); City of Bristol Record Office (owned by City Council): 22 (01250(1)); British Museum, London: 53 (MLA 92,5-1,1); from P. Drach, *Spiegel der Menschen Behaltniss*: 2; from Early English Text Society, *Bubees Book*, 1868: 18; (from Gregory's *Moralia*, Latin 15675, f.8v, Bibliothèque Nationale): 23; from *Herbolario Volgare*, 1692: 56; Michael Holford: 5, 6, 10; Henry E. Huntingdon Library, San Morino, California: 17 (British Library facsimile Vol. 1, f.51); Musée Condé, Chantilly: 44 and front cover (MS 65/1284, f.1v. Photo for front cover supplied by Giraudon); Museo Civico Medievale, Bologna. Photo CNB&C: 29 (MS 641, f.1r); Elizabeth Eames, drawn by Rosemonde Nairac: 25, 51; from Tapestry at Nancy, Lorraine: 43; Österreichische National-bibliothek, Vienna: 27 (Codex Vindobensis Series Nova 2644, f.53); Visual Publications Ltd: 11; Kate Rogers: 14, 15, 19, 26, 31, 33, 35, 49, 55 and the line drawings on pp. 19, 30, 36, 39, 41, 43, 54, 63, 64, 72, 78, 106, 121, 138; Trinity College, Cambridge: 58 (MS 0.1.20, f.165).

SUBJECT INDEX OF OLD RECIPES

INDEX

References in *italic* refer to the pages on which illustrations appear.